The American Drama Since 1930

ESSAYS ON PLAYWRIGHTS
AND PLAYS

by

JOSEPH MERSAND, Ph.D.

KENNIKAT PRESS, INC./PORT WASHINGTON, N. Y.

To

E. J. H.

THE AMERICAN DRAMA SINCE 1930

Copyright, 1949, by Joseph Mersand
Reissued 1968 by Kennikat Press by arrangement

Library of Congress Catalog Card No: 68-26238
Manufactured in the United States of America

ESSAY AND GENERAL LITERATURE INDEX REPRINT SERIES

THE AMERICAN DRAMA
SINCE 1930

ESSAYS ON PLAYWRIGHTS
AND PLAYS

CONTENTS

PREFACE

The eight essays in this volume were written for *THE PLAYERS MAGAZINE* at the invitation of Mrs. A. B. Joder, the editor. The writer is grateful for the opportunity to express his views on the contemporary drama in the pages of the magazine and for the permission to reprint them now. The American drama of the past two decades has assumed such an important position in the drama of the world, that it is time to reflect on the phenomenon. Amidst many rapid changes which we have witnessed, we have also become aware that the dramatic capital of the world has shifted to New York City.

Critical evaluations of the contemporary drama appear with considerable frequency. In the last few years substantial volumes have come from the pens of such noted critics as Joseph Wood Krutch, Anita Block, Burns Mantle, John Mason Brown, Eleanor Flexner, William Kozlenko, John W. Gassner, and Frank H. O'Hara. There can be no end, of course, to such studies as long as our drama is constantly being replenished at the rate of about two hundred plays a season, and as long as we are free from the deadening censorship which has practically destroyed the dramatic output in Europe.

The four dramatists discussed have not all come of age during these years, but have definitely become international figures during that period. George S. Kaufman and Elmer Rice have been criticized and analyzed almost for the past twenty years, and little can now be said which has not been said before. In the essays on Clare Boothe and Clifford Odets, the writer has attempted to record his impressions gained at first-hand from attendance at each of the plays of these two dramatists, whose careers he has followed from their initial dramatic efforts.

The four aspects of the American drama which constitute the second half of the book are attempts at summarizing certain tendencies of the past two decades. Unless there is some organization, some discernment of unity in the diversity of plays that are produced, each season will resemble the other, and our critical faculties will have no occasion for use.

The past two decades in the American drama have been rich enough to deserve a more thorough treatment, one that would be carefully documented and replete with footnotes. The present writer has not attempted to make such a complete study. The four playwrights he has evaluated might easily have been four hundred others. The four tendencies he has noted might have been enlarged to include a score of others. If these essays contribute to a richer appreciation of our drama or to a more thorough understanding of the intentions and achievements of certain of our dramatists, they will deserve their reproduction in book form.

The original collection of these essays in book form appeared in 1941 under the title *The American Drama 1930-1940*, and is now out-of-print. To meet the continuing demand for copies, the writer has completely revised the contents and brought all references up to date. Since the original title would not refer to the plays discussed from 1941-1948, the present title, *The American Drama Since 1930*, has been selected as indicating more accurately the scope of the volume.

J. M.

PART ONE

PLAYWRIGHTS

George S. Kaufman

MASTER OF TECHNIQUE

GEORGE S. Kaufman's *The Late George Apley* was his thirty-sixth play written in collaboration. Though critics may argue as to the ultimate value of his plays in the history of American drama, they almost unanimously agree that he is our most successful collaborator working in the theatre. His associates have included Irving Pichel, Larry Evans, Marc Connelly, Edna Ferber, Katherine Dayton, Alexander Woollcott, Moss Hart, Ring Lardner, and Morrie Ryskind. The only play he wrote alone was *The Butter and Egg Man* (1925).

Superlatives of various kinds have been used with Kaufman. He is generally recognized as the most successful master of stage technique in our contemporary theatre. He is acknowledged as our outstanding satirist, one of our best directors, one of the best writers of dialogue, and as our most capable "play-doctor." If degrees *honoris causa* were awarded for technical efficiency in drama as they are for skill in operative surgery or quantitative analysis, Kaufman would have been honored by at

21

least the same number of universities which have graduated Dr. Nicholas Murray Butler, late President of Columbia University.

The surprising thing about his wizardry on the stage is that he had already been credited with it twenty years ago when he wrote *The Royal Family* with Edna Ferber. Since that time, when critics thought that he had reached his peak, he has developed in the versatility of his technique, in the depth of his social consciousness, in the sparkle and wit of his satire, and in his understanding of human nature. For Kaufman has not stood still. Basing his plays on the occurrences in his immediate environment, he has been compelled to change his technique, his subject-matter, and his point of view with each new production. Consequently he has become unpredictable. His many admirers have come to expect a good and even exceptional evening in the theatre, but their expectations are never as delightful as their experiences with the realities. Kaufman's play, *The Man Who Came to Dinner*, marked his twentieth anniversary as a dramatist, and his two decades of labor are well worth a new evaluation.

Kaufman's personal development has run parallel to that of American drama in general. Twenty-five years ago, we had plays which were either diluted imitations of Continental and British successes or insipid pipings in the wind. Louis Anspacher's *The Unchastened Woman* was considered a significant study of the modern woman and Eugene Walters' *The Easiest Way* was a bold venture in the study of morals. It is doubtful whether either play could endure a successful revival.

Today our drama is watched by alert playgoers everywhere. Eugene O'Neill, Maxwell Anderson, S. N. Behrman, George S. Kaufman, Rose Franken, Elmer Rice, Philip Barry, and dozens of other American playwrights have seen their plays produced on the stage from Stockholm to Vienna. Maxwell Anderson's *Elizabeth the Queen* won over the critical audience of Vienna, Eugene O'Neill's *Strange Interlude* was acclaimed in Stockholm, John Wexley's *Steel* was successful in Moscow, and Allan Boretz's *Room Service* was a hit in London.

Even though *You Can't Take It With You* was a failure in London, the circumstance was the occasion of lengthy comment by critics here and abroad. Kaufman's success has been so remarkable in New York that his failure in London seemed incredible. All sorts of explanations were made. Charles Morgan, writing from London, J. B. Priestley, writing in

New York and Brooks Atkinson, drama critic of the *New York Times,* covered almost the entire front page of the Sunday drama section of the *New York Times* in discussing the London debacle.

The career of Kaufman is similar to that of many dramatists of today: journalist, columnist, dramatic critic, dramatist. Such has been the experience of George Ade, Ring Lardner, and S. N. Behrman, all of whom came to the stage after a career in journalism. Kaufman was born in Pittsburgh in 1889. After graduating from the public high school, he studied law for a few months but finally gave it up because he found it too difficult. His occupations were numerous and various and brought him into contact with all sorts of human beings who undoubtedly enriched his understanding of human nature. He worked as a chainman and as a transit man on a surveying corps, a window clerk in the Allegheny county tax office, a stenographer, and a travelling salesman.

In 1908 he came to New York and began his literary career as a volunteer contributor to Franklin P. Adams' column in *The Evening Mail.* Through Adams' help he secured the position as a columnist on Frank Munsey's *Washington Times* (1912-1913). Although Kaufman thought the column humorous, his employer seems to have disagreed with him. A year later Kaufman succeeded to Adams' column when his mentor joined the staff of the *Herald-Tribune*.

From writing for a humorous column to reporting on the new plays was an easy step. Kaufman eventually became dramatic editor of the *New York Times*. Every dramatic critic, as some disappointed playwright has said, is either an unsuccessful or an expectant dramatist. Kaufman's interest in the practical side of the theatre was not long in developing.

About this time, Henry R. Stern of the Joseph W. Stern Music Company, formed an organization for the encouragement of young playwrights. Kaufman, who was recommended for his promise, submitted a check-raising farce called *Going Up*. The play was never produced but among those who read it and admired its snappy dialogue and comic situations was John Peter Toohey, at that time an associate of George C. Tyler, the producer. Toohey suggested Kaufman's possibilities to Tyler, and Kaufman was soon working on *Dulcy*.

Before his writing of *Dulcy* (1921) Kaufman had collaborated with Irving Pichel on *The Failure,* which never reached production. With the late Larry Evans he wrote *Someone in the House* (1918), which was unsuccessful. The writing of

Dulcy deserves detailed treatment, because it is one of those plays whose genesis is well known and is an illuminating insight into dramatic creation.

George C. Tyler needed a comedy for Lynn Fontanne, Ellen Terry's brilliant protégé. Kaufman and Marc Connelly were invited to write a play using material which had appeared in Franklin P. Adams' column in the *Herald-Tribune* in 1914. Kaufman has described its composition thus:

"We had a great break of luck with it —the various parts fell into place all in one Sunday afternoon." It was fairly successful in New York, which was in a receptive frame of mind in the early twenties to plays deriding low I. Q.'s Only a year later Lewis's *Babbitt* appeared. Outside of New York the audiences were colder. Sophistication had barely reached the peripheries of the large cities. Not until another decade could satire and social criticism in plays succeed in such preliminary testing-grounds as Boston and Baltimore. Now Kaufman prefers to have his latest plays open out of town. *I'd Rather Be Right* put the Bostonians in quite a turmoil, and then Kaufman knew he had nothing to fear. When *Bring on the Girls* appeared to be sending them homewards in Baltimore and in Washington, the play folded up and never reached Broadway.

Since Kaufman's wit is essentially the kind which takes one by surprise because of its appropriateness and its felicity of phrase, will the same wit amuse an audience the second time? Nothing is so boring as a wise-crack endlessly repeated. Kaufman is perfectly aware of the immediacy of appeal of his plays as his well-known remark about his opinion of satire indicates. When questioned why he did not write satire more consistently instead of his popular plays with a touch of satire, he is said to have answered: "Satire is what closes Saturday night."

There is no doubt of his popular success. After his happy experience with Marc Connelly in 1921, he lost no time in writing *To the Ladies* and *Merton of the Movies* in 1922.

The following year they wrote two more plays, *The Deep Tangled Wildwood*, an exposure of New York's sophistication, which was a failure. Ten years later, with Edna Ferber, Kaufman tried again with the same theme in *Dinner at Eight*, a mordant criticism of Park Avenue society-folk. In 1923, Kaufman wrote his first book for a musical comedy, *Helen of Troy, New York*. *Be Yourself* (1924) *The Cocoanuts* (1925), *Strike Up the Band* (1927), *Animal Crackers* (1928), *The Band Wagon*

(1931), *Of Thee I Sing* (1931), *Let 'Em Eat Cake* (1933), *I'd Rather Be Right* (1937), and *Park Avenue* (1946) are other musical comedies for which he has fashioned the plots.

A dramatist deserves more than passing mention when his works achieve not merely a success of the moment but enrich the art-form, remove its limitations, and open new fields in which it may flourish. Has Kaufman been more than a wizard of stage-technique? Are his many popular successes readable, and "revivable"? The two Pulitzer prices for *Of Thee I Sing* and *You Can't Take It With You* indicate at least a certain estimable committee's testimony to his merit. To the historian of the drama, perhaps his two outstanding achievements have been *Of Thee I Sing* and *I'd Rather Be Right*.

Of the first it might truly be said that it was a pioneer-effort. Critics thought that they had touched the zenith of adulation when they spoke of it as the nearest American counterpart to the Gilbert and Sullivan operettas. Yet *Of Thee I Sing* was even superior to the immortal Savoy operettas in certain respects. There is about such productions as *Pinafore*, *Iolanthe* and *Ruddigore* a feeling of gayety, yes, but also a childish kind of gayety. To make sophisticates laugh, to have tickled the mind, not the ribs, that was Kaufman's feat. To wring a laugh out of the war debt tangle; to have made a Presidential campaign exciting before the 1932 and 1936 battles; to have dared to present the Nine Old Men on the stage in an attitude more prejudicial than judicial; to have taken the dullness out of politics and to have substituted laughter — that was something new in American drama. Kaufman found so much in American life to ridicule, because there are so many foibles and follies that deserve only ridicule. Tin Pan Alley was the subject for his satire in *June Moon* (1929); the stupidities of the moguls of Hollywood were ridiculed in *Once in a Lifetime* (1930); joiners were told some unpleasant things in *The Good Fellow;* and the Republicans surely were satisfied with the criticism of the New Deal in *I'd Rather Be Right.*

As a satirist of the more obvious stupidities and crudities of American Life, Kaufman is easily the master. His training as a columnist twenty-five years ago has made him a kind of dramatic column-writer, writing flippantly about things that have amused him. No one expects a well-thought-out philosophy of life from such a writer, any more than one expects Walter Winchell or Louis Sobol to be included in a revision of Will Durant's

Story of Philosophy. Yet no man of intelligence living in such times as these can have failed to adopt certain definite ideas about artistic, economic and social problems.

Kaufman's artistic philosophy is perhaps most clearly stated in *Merrily We Roll Along,* written with Moss Hart in 1934. The dramatic device of beginning a play with the present and then retreating into the past was effective, to be sure, but after all, only a dramaturgic trick. To many observers this story of the commercialization of an idealistic young playwright seemed something in the nature of a confession on Kaufman's part. Certainly no American dramatist would understand the emotions of a successful dramatist whose millions do not satisfy his artistic cravings. The conquest of dollars over idealism has often been treated by our dramatists, but never with the poignancy and irony which Kaufman gave to his play. The times may have influenced the dramatist, for a few years later he was back to broad comedy. His excursion into the field of literary art and its difficulties is one of the truly revealing contributions to this difficult subject.

What is Kaufman's general philosophy of life? Has he any ideas? Will he eventually join the immortals, or is he just another successful dramatist, another Kotzebue, a Scribe, a Boucicault? Mere technical proficiency never made an enduring playwright. Is Kaufman satisfied with his financial returns and content, to leave dramatic Art to his younger contemporaries?

In the opinion of Joseph Wood Krutch, drama critic of *The Nation*, Kaufman has not a consistent point of view. "He has said a hundred witty things; he is certainly on the side of good sense; yet it would be very difficult after reading his twenty-odd plays to say that they tend in any direction."[1] Since this statement was made fifteen years ago, certain plays have appeared in which ideas are important. These are *Merrily We Roll Along* (1934), *First Lady* (1935), *Stage Door* (1936), *You Can't Take It With You* (1936), *I'd Rather Be Right* (1937), and *The Fabulous Invalid* (1939). Sometimes Kaufman's point of view is one of good common sense, such as expressed by Grandpa Vanderhof in *You Can't Take It With You*. Briefly, his philosophy of life is one of enjoying it while one can. Perhaps Kaufman, who knows what the public wants, gave them their own land of heart's

---

[1] "The Random Satire of George S. Kaufman," *The Nation*, August 9, 1933, 156-8.

desire. In our nerve-wrecking civilization we all crave a Shangri-La, a haven of refuge.

Kaufman's philosophy of life may not be consistent, not even positive, but it is quite evident and animates his plays. In all his satires and comedies with satirical flavors he shows his refusal to be fooled by the things which befuddle most people. His superiority to other writers like Sinclair Lewis and H. L. Mencken, who likewise have capitalized on their clarity of vision, lies in his ability to preserve that attitude when the others have succumbed.

Kaufman has shown Americans how ridiculous some of their most cherished institutions are: their rotary clubs, their hypocritical adoration of women, their thirst for the dollar, their worship of material success. To have become successful by condemning the pet notions of his audience is an unusual accomplishment. It was said of a certain performance of *You Can't Take It With You* that one of the spectators laughed so heartily that he fell off a balcony and yet was unharmed. There is something symbolic in that. Kaufman has turned some of America's most sacred prejudices upside down, but their possessors have survived the experience. Perhaps it does us much good to see the world sometimes standing on our heads. Kaufman may be able to stand on his feet and see what a crazy, silly, yet happy world this is. Our age demands more people with eyes that cannot be fooled by superficialties, with minds which can sum up the absurdities of a situation in an epigram, with courage to laugh at the weaknesses of men, be they movie moguls or Presidents.

Elmer Rice

REALIST OF THE DRAMA

CERTAIN writers have become associated with definite areas, rural and urban, which always influence their books: Thomas Hardy and Wessex, Arnold Bennett and the English Pottery District, Ben Hecht and Chicago, Mary E. W. Freeman and New England, Schnitzler and pre-War Vienna, Maupassant and Paris. Elmer Rice has been the interpreter of New York. His long novel, *Imperial City,* is the most complete picture of the metropolis ever attempted, and many have been the attempts. In 1900, enough novels had been written about New York to warrant the publication of *New York in Fiction* by Arthur Bartlett Maurice.

Of all the numerous plays about poor New York, Rice's *Street Scene* (1929) is probably the most convincing. Rice has not confined his playwriting to Manhattan, although his best work was done when he was concerned with it. His drama, *Between Two Worlds* (1934), took place on an Atlantic liner going to Europe. *Judgment Day* (1934) was a story laid in some central European country though it was obviously a dramatization of the trial of

Dimitroff for the burning of the German Reichstag. *The Left Bank* (1931) had Paris as its setting. Yet critics will agree that he has been most successful when he described New York and its inhabitants, in *Street Scene* (1929), in *Counsellor-at-Law* (1931), in his various plays concerned with the law.

Rice's study of law may explain his qualities as a playwright. Almost from his first play to the last he has exhibited a passionate hatred for injustice, which at times worked to the detriment of his dramaturgy. He has always been admired for the marvelous accuracy of his observation of little, though vitally characteristic, details. New Yorkers experienced many pleasures in *Street Scene* and in *Counsellor-at-Law* which were denied to a visitor. These were due to his power to recognize characters by the appropriateness of their speech, their dress, their mannerisms of deportment. George Arliss in his autobiography, *Up From Bloomsbury*, mentions one of his earliest successes in creating the illusion of reality. He had the simple assignment of walking into an office, placing his hat upon a hat-rack and then beginning his day's work as an ordinary clerk advanced in years. Arliss put so much study into this part, through observation as well as intuition that he always earned applause as he executed this

Elmer Rice's plays abound in mar
cameos of portraiture. *Street Sce*
forty-three characters, most of them ...
delineated and clearly differentiated.
Counsellor-at-Law and *We, the People*
also had large casts which required large
rôles, not mere "stooge parts."

Equally apparent throughout his plays,
in addition to his love for justice and his
accuracy of observation is his sensitivity
to and dislike for the more material aspects
of contemporary American civilization. In
his first play, *The Subway,* which was not
produced until *Street Scene* became a hit,
he describes the wearying effects of the
daily office routine upon a sensitive young
girl. In this respect it antedated Sophie
Treadwell's *Machinal,* which was one of
the best plays of 1928. *The Adding Machine* (1923), which was produced by the
Theatre Guild, was an allegory of a young
man's travail in a business civilization
which had little respect for individual
personalities.

As long as Rice confined himself to
demonstrating the tragic implications of
industrialization and commercialization,
critics were willing to accept him. They
had the precedents of Galsworthy's *Justice,*
of the plays of Shaw and his imitators, of
the young dramatists of the Twenties and

the O'Neill of *Beyond the Horizon*. When Rice, after his great success with *Counsellor-at-Law*, an assortment of portraits in a metropolitan law office, tried to present his vision of the disintegrating effect of the depression, critics abandoned him. They had expected another series of portraits and not a passionate outburst against prejudiced judges, company-unions, unscrupulous employers, and other unpleasant features of Big Business. The following year Rice's anger at the persecution in Nazi Germany led him to portray the Reichstag Fire Trial in which such characters as Gœring, Hitler, and Van der Lubbe appeared. The New York critics were even more dissatisfied. Granting that Rice was within his rights as a dramatist to be angry with the Nazis, they denied him the privilege of using the stage as a soap-box against Nazism.

Here, they said, was a melodramatic harangue, not a play. Rice was accustomed to unfavorable criticism, and went ahead with the presentation of another play that same year. This time the critics' disapproval proved too much and *Between Two Worlds* closed quickly.

His refusal to compromise with his principles caused trouble a year later when he resigned his position as New York City Director of the Federal Theatre Project because the Government refused to permit the first edition of the Living Newspaper to include Mussolini and Haile Selassie.

One may admire a man's courage in facing his adversaries undaunted and yet admit that he is an inefficient dramatist. That seems to explain the critics' attitude. It does not explain Elmer Rice's respect for the power of the critics, for these two plays failed not because the critics disliked them but because the public was disappointed. Rice knew as well as any man in the theatre that any number of plays have become pronounced successes after universal condemnation by the reviewers. One always likes to mention *Abie's Irish Rose* and its competitor for the long-run record, *Tobacco Road*.

One explanation for the lukewarm reception to his last few plays is found in the unpreparedness of the New York audiences. Only two years after *We, the People*, Clifford Odets' *Waiting for Lefty* made its astonishing appearance. Plays of social significance were wanted. The *Theatre Union* was born in 1933 and could offer such tendentious dramas as *Peace on Earth*, *Stevedore*, *The Black Pit*, and *Sailors of Cattaro*. Could *Pins and Needles* and *The Cradle Will Rock* have been hits in 1932? It is extremely unlikely. Rice's was that pioneering effort which seems always destined to fail because of its strangeness.

To-day in reading this early dramatic study of the American depression, one cannot help admiring the courage of its author. Rice in 1931 had written a great popular and critical success. Perhaps only the appearance of *Of Thee I Sing* in the same season took the Pulitzer Prize out of his hands. He knew enough of New York (his novel *Imperial City* has enough plots for ten plays) to have produced another colorful *genre* painting. Yet he chose to do something entirely different. Time will tell whether Rice lost himself as a dramatist while he found himself as a campaigner for social justice. Perhaps Rice should have written a satire and thus have won the audiences which thronged to *The Cradle Will Rock* and *Pins and Needles*. It is not charasteristic of him to descend to comedy simply because it is easier to accept than drama. When comedy appears in his plays it usually derives from the characters. The mother of Mr. Simon, the district leader, the gum-chewing stenographer, all of *Counsellor-at-Law;* the Italian janitor, the Russian socialist of *Street Scene*—these are comic characters because they are human and the verisimilitude of their portrait provokes one to the laughter of recognition, a frequent experience in the theatre.

Has Elmer Rice made any distinguished contributions to American drama, or is he another successful dramatist popular for the moment, meriting but a paragraph in the history of American drama of the twentieth century? For out of an average season in New York when about two hundred plays are produced, Burns Mantle selects ten for his annual collection. Most often these are the most significant plays of the season. Have Rice's plays fared well with Mr. Mantle, for a test of excellence of some value is the inclusion in the annual volume. *Street Scene* was included in the 1928 volume and *The Left Bank* in 1931. It must be admitted that Rice is no Kaufman whose latest hit almost invariably meets Mr. Mantle's requirements.

Certain gifts of characterization have been revealed by Rice, which incline one to the belief that on the permanence of these characters will depend his reputation. In the theatre one easily comes under their spell and is quite willing to believe in their existence. Rice knows the souls of several people and can describe many more. Thus his portrait of Simon, counsellor-at-law, is probably his masterpiece. Having worked in law offices, knowing the personality of the Jewish professional whose parents were humble immigrants as well as any practising dramatist, Rice naturally excels in such portraits. The mother of Simon, with her pardonable pride in her son's prominence, with her constant expression "I've got plenty of time" is a living portrait. Not many dramatists have succeeded in creating such characters.

With the dramatist's keen eye for the revealing detail, Rice can create a character by giving her a distinctive walk. Thus in *Counsellor-at-Law* one of the secretaries had a gait the like of which had not been seen on the stage. She walked as if all the sense of weariness and unappreciated excellence were locked up in her heart. Whenever she appeared the audience was amused. It may have been merely a dramatic trick, but it was effective.

Next in importance among his significant contributions is his skill in interpreting sections of New York life. Among the favorite topics of discussion among playgoers when *Street Scene* was the hit of the town was the exact location of the street described. Some observers went so far as to photograph three-storied houses which they were certain were the originals of the one in the play. Only Rice's statement that his picture was a generalization of the many brownstone houses in Manhattan put an end to the discussion. The eagerness of the debaters was an indication that "willing suspension of disbelief" wh Coleridge said was so necessary for col plete enjoyment in the theatre. Very fe stage-pictures of the ordinary daily life i New York City can compare with *Street Scene*.

As a dramatist of social justice, however, Elmer probably prefers to be judged. To be sure he is in great company including Bernard Shaw, John Galsworthy, Gerhart Hauptmann, Sean O'Casey, to mention but a few of the greatest in the field.

Alexandre Dumas *fils's* doctrine that art should be for man's sake motivates these writers. These authors do not weigh out their emotions, being careful that their indignation does not overbalance their sense of the dramatic. Sometimes, as was the case of Galsworthy, whose temperament was more under control, the indignation will be perceived by the spectators rather than smeared all over the play. It is ridiculous, of course, to chastise Rice because his temperament is unlike Galsworthy's and hence causes him sometimes to shout when the restrained Englishman might use understatement.

It is to Rice's credit that he refused to curry popular approval merely by turning out acceptable realistic portraits simply because these had proven successful. What places Rice into the higher category of American dramatists is his refusal to confine himself to one successful type of play. Like O'Neill, who has been constantly experimenting with new forms, Rice used different techniques. In *The Adding Machine* he tried expressionism at a time when it was the "last word" in continental drama. In *We, the People,* particularly in the last act, Rice took the audience into his confidence as he made it the jury before whom his hero is tried.

Finally, Rice is one of the brave fighters using the vehicle of the stage. He is not a propagandist preaching universal unionization as a solution of the economic ills of our time, or a revolution from the right or the left. He preaches *against* rather than *for.* He is against oppression, whether he finds it in Germany or in a mid-Western American town, or in Czarist Russia. He is alive to the beauties of the world, one of which, young love, is tenderly portrayed in several plays. He has written about the ugliness of our impersonal business civilization which makes possible such tragedies as he described in *The Adding Machine, Street Scene,* and *We, the People.*

His novel, *Imperial City,* is an enlarged play such as he might have written if he had a week of nights in which to present it. His talent in revealing character by significant details enables him to present such a vast array of characters, most of whom are convincing in their verisimilitude. It represents in some respects the climax of his achievement as the portrayer of New York. His social conciousness, his clear eye which enables him to see corruption in politics as well as in family life, his sympathy for a man of good taste, Professor Coleman, his awareness of the thousand and one sights and sounds of the city, they are all characteristic of the Elmer Rice who began his remarkable literary career with *On Trial* (1914), which was a triumph for the author and a veritable gold mine for Arthur Hopkins who produced it.

What direction will Rice take now? The grievances which inspired him to significant dramas are still existent and many new ills have arisen since 1914. An artist who has been stimulated once must create or lose the name of artist. Whether Rice will use the novel or the play, we can be certain that his work will result from careful observation, from intellectual honesty which cannot be bribed by popular acclaim or browbeaten by governmental edict, from a passionate hatred for brutality, stupidity, and ugliness, and from an unflinching desire to portray the truth that ought to set slaves free.

Clare Boothe

WOMAN'S GIFT TO DRAMATIC SATIRE

ALTHOUGH Clare Boothe had written only two successful plays up to June 8, 1939, it is significant that Richard Lockridge, dramatic critic of the *New York Sun*, listed her among leading American playwrights in his article, "The American Theatre of Today," written for the United States Number of the *London Times*. He placed her in a class which included Maxwell Anderson, Clifford Odets, Robert Sherwood, Philip Barry, Lillian Hellman, Elmer Rice, and George S. Kaufman.

There is one sentence in the same article that might well serve as the text of any discussion of Miss Boothe as a dramatist.

"The English reviewers seem generally to regard the American Theatre as adolescent. It has, just now at any rate, some of the seriousness of adolescence, and a good deal of the confusion. It is not really paradoxical to add that it has been, for the past decade and for the first time in its history, talking, at its best, about things which can interest adults."

Clare Boothe's plays are written for the adult intelligence. *The Women* has been called by some "The most brilliant social satire of its time."[1] Satires are not popular with adolescents. It is as a social satirist that this study will present Miss Boothe. George S. Kaufman undoubtedly possesses a greater knowledge of theatrical craftsmanship. S. N. Behrman's polished sallies are probably more quotable and more permanent. Rachel Crothers and Edna Ferber probably understand more clearly and present the female character with greater verisimilitude.

Yet Clare Boothe, even with her meager output of only three plays, has already assumed an important position among the leading American dramatists. *The Women* is one of the frankest studies of the sex penned by one of its members. To say, as so many male critics have, that Miss Boothe wrote so acidly because she despised the representatives of the set she presented, is hardly as important as the fact that she had the courage, rare even in a male writer, to present women unfavorably. H. L. Mencken, John Macy, John Langdon-Davies, John Erskine, Havelock Ellis, and W. L. George have all expostulated upon

---

[1] Burns Mantle, *Contemporary American Playwrights,* New York, Dodd Mead, 1938, p. 171.

the strengths and weaknesses of the *Daughters of Eve*. But a deeply-inbred, typically American respect for the sex (the save the women and children first idea) would always prevent any male writer from writing as bitterly as he might want. The spirit of chivalry is still strong. No man, even though he might want to, would have dared to have been so caustic in his satire. Neither would he have been accepted. His view would have been considered prejudiced, colored by his own misadventures, and thoroughly condemned. Miss Boothe, being of the same sex, firmly established in the Park Avenue set, married to wealthy Henry R. Luce, editor of TIME, FORTUNE, and LIFE, can afford to say what she thinks.

No one can tell her to return to the backward country from which she came, where women are so low in man's opinion. She does not depend on her plays for her daily sustenance and so can afford to run the risk of offending large potential blocs of stay-at-homers. Her financial position precludes any criticism of her views as a radical bent on undermining the social *status quo*. Whether or not she has been aware of her immunity against charges that would be hurled at a man writing her type of play, she has profited from the favorable set of circumstances.

Social satire is not the most popular type

of play, and seldom does it win fame and fortune for its author. It was 'George S. Kaufman, author of so many hits, who defined satire as "that which closes Saturday night." In his early years as a dramatist, he, too, contributed his share to the slim treasury of American masterpieces of satire. *Dulcy, To The Ladies, Once in a Lifetime,* all are satires. In recent years he has been content with such comedies as *The Man Who Came To Dinner, You Can't Take It With You,* and *George Washington Slept Here,* which filled the till of the box-office but which could offend few.

Consider the amazing courage—or is it recklessness—of the woman who attacks her entire sex in one play, the motion picture industry in a second, and the inanities of the Nazi government in a third. *Kiss the Boys Good-Bye* and *Margin for Error* do not have the sting of *The Women,* but they possess the same keen intellectual delights for theatre-goers who relish wit, clarity of judgment, and courageous things clearly expressed. In these days of muddled thinking generally a dramatist with a definite point of view and the cleverness to express it is a rare delight.

Those who are interested in knowing Miss Boothe's views on women, Hollywood, Fascism, and Nazism, need not rely on the plays themselves, for they have given even acute critics wrong ideas. The prefaces to Miss Boothe's printed plays must be read, and delightful reading they make indeed. Her preface to *The Women* is a defense of her attitude toward the specially selected Park Avenue Set delineated in the play..Her preface to *Kiss The Boys Good-bye* is one of the cleverest exposés of potential American Fascism yet written, and as such deserves a reprinting and a distribution at least to all preservers of Americanism.

Rare indeed is the dramatist who will inform his hearers or later his readers what his actual intentions were in any particular play. Most of them would prefer to keep their audiences guessing for thus the play would be under discussion and the box-office receipts will quickly reveal the effects of the added publicity. Who has not heard by this time of the early career of *Tobacco Road,* longest running American play? It was playing to practically empty houses until some college professor called it the worst play he ever saw. Then the crowds began to come.

Clare Boothe is too honest in her views to permit her public to remain in ignorance of her intentions. When she was excoriated by critics and by officers of women's clubs for her treatment of the feminine sex, she replied, in her preface to the printed play:

"*The Women* is a satirical play about a numerically small group of ladies native to the Park Avenues of America . . . the reader, who, warned of this, nevertheless claims to discover in it a portrait of all womankind, is obviously bound to experience the paradoxical discomfort which ensues to the wearer when the shoe unexpectedly fits."

The opprobrious epithets that greeted this socialite, former associate editor of VANITY FAIR, and contributor to a book on backgammon, reminded the student of the insults hurled in the British papers at Ibsen when his *Ghosts* was produced. Yet Miss Boothe took them graciously. Although the late Heywood Broun had called *The Women* one of the most unpleasant plays he had ever witnessed, she invited him to write an introduction to *Kiss The Boys Good-Bye*. Even this introduction did not agree with the author's own intentions, and she disagreed with it in her preface.

The success of *The Women* exceeded her fondest expectations, and she donated the profits to her favorite charities. Miss Boothe does not have to worry about box-office receipts, although as an artist she is more pleased with the public's approval than with its condemnation. She has known failure in the drama, as her first play, *Abide With Me* (1935), is better forgotten. Yet even in this failure some of the distinguishing marks of the later satirist can be discerned. Coming from The Park Avenue Set, which she knows so well, it is not surprising that her first play dealt with a depraved specimen of that set, in the form of a sadistic husband, who is finally shot by his childhood nurse. John Anderson, critic of the *Journal-American*, was representitive of the critics in his statement:

> "*Abide With Me* is a peculiarly uncomfortable play, so admirably done by a cast of slick actors, that its wobbly structure is almost hidden in the performance."

The wobbly structure was corrected in *The Women* two years later. This play revealed an original talent, the most gifted feminine satirist in the whole history of American drama. Yet a satirist must be a clear thinker and Miss Boothe's brilliant dialogue gave no hint of the troubled social analyst. *Kiss the Boys Goodbye* (1938) was intended by its author as an analysis of our contemporary society, with particular emphasis on the dangers of its succumbing to Fascism in the guise of Southernism or some other fancy American name. Even such a clear thinker as Heywood Broun thought that Miss Boothe was ridiculing Hollywood's vulgar ballyhoo in its search for the perfect Scarlett O'Hara. We discover to our surprise that Miss Boothe had a more serious motive, the uncovering of the similarity between foreign Fascism and our native brand as it has, in her opinion, been practised in the South since the beginnings of the Ku Klux Klan. In fact, she remarks, the colored shirt idea may have been borrowed from the white sheet of the Klansmen.

This revelation from Miss Boothe was, to put it mildly, amazing. Here was the wife of a wealthy editor, who was himself being mentioned as a sympathizer of Fascist ideals, attacking their presence within our own country. Needless to say, hardly a playgoer got that impression, and Miss Boothe was frightfully disappointed. Perhaps she should have written her exposition earlier in the play's history. To the student of the theatre, that expression of her fear of Fascism coming to America under some patriotic label revealed a personality, not only unaffected by her experience in the Park Avenue Set but acutely aware of our greatest political problem — the preservation of our democracy in a world of growing dictatorships.

Clare Bothe's introduction to *Kiss the Boys Goodbye* should be reprinted as a political tract. It packs more political wisdom than most of the pseudo-sagacities promulgated by highly-paid and highly-praised feminine commentators.

Her next play followed naturally. *Margin for Error* is a "satirical melodrama," to use her own words. It is the most bitter condemnation of Nazi-inspired characters since the Nazi regime assumed power. Since Hitler's advent almost a score of plays have been presented on the New York Stage in which Nazi brutalities were uncovered. The dramatists were among our best. Elmer Rice's *Judgment Day* (1935), although it was a failure in New York, had a very successful run in London. Clifford Odets in 1936 wrote a bitter one-acter, *Till the Day I Die*. Katherine Dayton, author of the successful *First Lady*, could not "ring the bell" with *Save Me the Waltz*. Leslie Reede's *The Shatter'd Lamp*, the first of the anti-Nazi plays to be produced (1933), had the dubious distinction of having been declined by the British censor as too offensive to the head of a foreign government. Those were the days of appeasement. It had a brief run of a month. Richard Maibaum, author of the comedy success of 1939, *See My Lawyer*, tried his hand at the problem with

Birthright (1933), but it failed. Samuel French thought enough of it to print the text.

Of all the plays that are anti-Nazi in tone, Clare Boothe's *Margin for Error* if not the most moving, at least was the most successful. Its action takes place in a German consulate in New York City. Characters introduced are the American Leader of the Bund, the consul's wife, who hates her husband and is afraid to leave him for fear of vengeance on her father in Czecho-Slovakia, an American journalist who loves her, and a policeman assigned to guard the consul. The latter is found dead at the end of the first act. The entire second act is devoted to discovering the murderer who was present in the room. Told simply, it seems like any other murder melodrama, but Clare Boothe manages to inject as brilliant an attack of Nazism's racial and political creeds as our drama has seen. The hero of the play, Moe Finklestein, who has the unhappy assignment of guarding the life of the consul, and then discovering that in spite of all his vigilance, the consul has been murdered, is made vivid and extremely sympathetic. Miss Boothe is too honest an observer to fail to see the tragic injustice committed by fanatic racial theorists, and her play becomes a poignant plea for fair-mindedness.

The record speed with which she placed this play into rehearsal, only four days after she submitted her script, because she felt that her play could not wait for the arrival of her first producer, Mr. Max Gordon, from Hollywood, reveals her concern for the message it conveys. It was completed on September 3, just a few days after the Germans bombed Polish cities. She was returning from a European Tour of Poland, Rumania, the Balkans, France, and England. Her observations have made her play ring true.

Satirical gifts have been granted to few of our women of the pen. Dorothy Parker comes to mind as the only parellel in verse and narrative prose to Clare Boothe. Even though Rachel Crothers has a much longer career as a dramatist, she is not distinguished primarily as a satirist. Satire presupposes a hatred for the object ridiculed which is generally not associated with the former President of the Stage Relief Fund and similar benevolent organizations. Clare Boothe does not hesitate to admit her hatreds.

"I did not like these women," she wrote in the foreword to *The Women*. "I liked them so little that I put them into this small Doomsday Book, in order to rid myself once and for all of their hauntingly ungracious images."

She hated just as vehemently Cindy Lou, her Southern heroine in *Kiss the Boys Goodbye.* Her dislike of Otto B. Horst, Bund Leader, and Consul Karl Baumer is not disguised. One cannot resist the temptation to compare her attitude with that of John Galsworthy. He, too, was independently wealthy. There was no apparent reason for his interest in securing justice for the lower classes in *The Silver Box,* in his deprecation of labor controversy in *Strife,* in his distrust of British penal institutions in *Justice,* and in racial prejudice in *Loyalties.* Yet he refused to follow in his father's footsteps and assume the legal mantle from his father's shoulders. His sympathies were too strong to be manacled by the prejudices of his social class, which would have told him that "all this is too bad, but there's nothing we can do about it." Galsworthy loved quality in human beings too much, as his superb short story, *Quality,* so eloquently reveals, to be blinded by the callous indifference and muddled thinking of his class. He saw through the whole false fabric of his class, and his *Forsyte Saga* and its later volumes opened the eyes of the world to the weaknesses as well as the strength, the shallowness as well as stolidity, the hypocracies as well as honesty of his class.

Somehow Clare Boothe has gone through a similar enlightenment. As one reads her gay chapters in a book on backgammon published in 1931 and then marvels at the clarity of her vision in her introduction to *Kiss the Boys Goodbye,* one feels that here, too, an author has burst the bonds of her social and financial set. She has not played "cricket" with her former associates by revealing them as the despicable creatures they truly are, but she has played fairly as a creative artist. "Art for man's sake," said Dumas *fils,* "is the duty of a dramatist." Clare Boothe, bitter satirist that she is, writes in behalf of a democratic and creative America. Only by annihilating the parasites at home and imported from abroad can she do most service to the cause of art. Her margin of error has been little, **indeed,** to date.

Clifford Odets

DRAMATIST OF YOUNG AMERICA

CLIFFORD ODETS' play, *Night Music,* lasted but two weeks, but it provoked more discussion than any of its predecessors. In the March 3, 1940, issue of the Drama Section of the *New York Times,* Brooks Atkinson devoted his weekly essay to an evaluation of the play while Harold Clurman, its director, expressed his favorable opinion. In fact, the author himself in the drama column of the *New York World-Telegram* on March 2, 1940, was permitted to act as drama critic and promptly attacked the critics. Notwithstanding this failure, Odets is one of the most promising figure in contemporary American drama. At thirty-three he saw his first six plays printed in a Modern Library collection, a tribute vouchsafed to very few contemporaries. Even though Brooks Atkinson disliked *Night Music,* he still admitted that Odets was "a man of extraordinary talents." Hardly a book appears these days on American drama without a discussion of Odets. These include Anita Block's *The Changing World in Plays and Theatre* (1939), Eleanor Flexner's *American Playwrights 1918-1938*

(1938), Joseph Wood Krutch *The American Drama Since 1918* (1939), Frank Hurburt O'Hara's *Today in American Drama* (1939), and John Mason Brown's *Two on the Aisle* (1939). Indispensable to the study of Odets is the Modern Library collection with its preface by the author and the three prefaces by Harold Clurman, who has directed all his plays.

What has Odets contributed to American drama that has earned him such extraordinary praise? Criticism has so far failed to determine the extent of his accomplishments. His plays merit a more extensive critical treatment than the daily reviewer has time or space for. His contributions to the drama of the depression need evaluation and classification. An intensive study of his plays, moreover, will prove fruitful to the student of literary inspiration and dramatic technique. For Clifford Odets has granted us the privilege of living through his own creative experiences from the original impulse to the completed work.

Such a revelation is not rare in the history of the literature of the drama. Grillparzer, Hebbel, Schiller, Gœthe, Shaw, and Ibsen, to mention but a few, have left us many notebooks of preliminary sketches, snatches of dialogue, outlines of plots, and other indications of their struggles for articulate expression. Odets, too, has told us how he wrote his plays, but he has gone one step further: he has told us why he wrote them. In several interviews and articles, he has expressed clearly and vividly his philosophy of life as well as his theories of drama. Asked to discuss the origin and purpose of *Awake and Sing*, he replied:

"Understand that I'm supposed to confess how I came to write *Awake and Sing!* I was sore; that's why I wrote that play. I was sore at my whole life. Getting nothing done. Stuffed in a room waiting for Luther Adler to perish so I might get a chance at playing his part in *Success Story*. All my life wondering whether to act or write. But all the time acting to make a living.

"When the Group came along, it began to mean more, but yet it was wrong for me. What could you do with a part in another fellow's play? Could you say something was wrong with people? Not much chance.

"You see, I read a lot of Emerson once. I heard a lot of Beethoven's last quartets. I looked at El Grecos. I got to have a pretty fine idea of what a man could be if he had a chance.

"But I saw (and I see it every day, all over the city) girls and boys were not getting a chance. I saw—make it the present—much terror in life. I went over my boyhood and tabulated the people's lives which had touched mine. I wrote small sketches on yellow paper, and when I read back I saw a strange and wonderful sort of *Spoon River Anthology*, but

63

deeper and more hurting to me because the memories were self-experienced.

"A young man in America tries to get away from himself—tries to cancel his own experience until it resembles more the general patterns. Certainly it is true of all the workers in creative things. Some escape the general trend. I began wrong. But now—in this little room—I saw where my own experience was richest, where it hurt me most, joyed me most. So I started on *Awake and Sing!* I read lines to fellow-actors who were living in the same apartment. We were all unhappy; we listened to phonograph music. I went on writing.

"Lee Strasberg moved downtown, and I moved with him. The last act was finished in his kitchen, on the bread board. I didn't like to work near him where he might be wakened. When I looked it over I saw I hadn't wanted to write exactly the play that came out. But it satisfied me; I saw there was material there enough to do better next time.

"The next time is over now. The new full-length one is called *Paradise Lost.* For me it spells farewell, Bronx. I'm looking at people in different places now. I've been around. Years in dramatic stock. A good play is there. Advertising offices. Another good play. Broadway—another good play. I only hope I live long enough to write out what I feel. Shortly I'm getting to the coal fields and the textile centers. Let New York see the rest of the country. Hollywood, too. Play material enough to keep six dozen writers going."[1]

Odets has answered many questions regarding his methods, his ideas on life as well as drama, and his purpose as a dra-

---

[1] *New York World-Telegram*, March 19, 1935.

matist. Odets' statement just quoted will help us understand the characters and motifs in his plays.

"I heard a lot of Beethoven's last quartets," he writes. That is why old Jacob Berger, the lovable grandfather in *Awake and Sing,* plays his phonograph when he is disappointed in America. That makes understandable Jacob's suicide when his ungrateful daughter breaks his records. For music is his consolation. Caruso, singing with joy in *L'Africane* as he sights land, reminds Jacob of his own joy when he beheld the shore of America, the land of his dreams and hopes. In *Till the Day I Die,* the leading character is a violinist; and mention is often made of the pleasure he took, together with other members of his family, in playing the quartets of Brahms. In *Golden Boy* Mr. Bonaparte wants his son Joe to be a violinist, to bring joy into the hearts of all people. On his twenty-second birthday Joe was to have received a $1,200 violin as a birthday gift. What follows is perhaps the most touching scene in the play. Joe refuses to take the violin with him on his Western boxing tour and his father denies him "the good word."

Another of Odets' statements is even more pertinent, because it represents the theme of all his plays: "I see it every day all over the city, girls and boys were not getting a chance." It is these people who never get a chance that interest the dramatist. Their frustrations, and their inferiority complexes arising from the frustrations, constitute the real subject-matter of Odets' plays. Certain critics have labeled him a propaganda playwright because of this preoccupation. How clearly the dramatist himself has answered them!

Waiting for Lefty had a functional value. This is sometimes called the propaganda angle in writing. But the important thing about *Awake and Sing* is the fact that the play stems first from real character, life and social background of these people.

It may be said that anything which one writes on "the side" of the large majority of people is propaganda. But today the truth followed to its logical conclusion is inevitably revolutionary. No special pleading is necessary in a play which says that people should have fuller and richer lives.[2]

What greater motif can any artist have? This is not "art for art's sake." This is "art for man's sake," in the words of Dumas *fils,* and later of John Galsworthy. This explains Shaw, the early Hauptmann, Ernst Toller, Franz Werfel, Schnitzler— and where could we end? Might it not be urged that great art today must be social as distinguished from mere self-expression ; that it must be aware of the submerged

[2] *New York World-Telegram,* March 19, 1935.

third and must do something about it?

The literature of the Gay Nineties, of the Yellow Book, holds no attraction for us today. Oscar Wilde and Max Beerbohm seem detached and lacking in vitality. The latter's *Happy Hypocrite* was dramatized recently and enjoyed a brief success. It was a delightful fantasy, something to escape to, but it did not stir the emotions as great drama has always done.

Millions are aware that boys and girls are "not getting a chance." But a dramatist must show the causes, the *roots;* and one who digs at the roots may by virtue of etymology be said to be a radical. The great American individualist Thoreau would have welcomed Odets for his getting at the roots of things; for did he not write in his *Walden* that a thousand were hacking at the branches of evil but only one was digging at the roots?

Realizing that Odets aims to show us the American saga of failure in contrast to the usual success stories, we are prepared to appreciate the means by which he achieves his goal. As a dramatist he must rely on character development and not on soap-box oratory to show us frustration, its causes and its tragic results.

With the exception of Chekhov, no other dramatist has brought together so many thwarted individuals in one play as there

are, for example, in *Waiting for Lefty*:
Dr. Benjamin (his father read Spinoza and
peddled shoe-laces for a living), a brilliant young chemist who refused to ex-
periment with poison gas; Joe, who is
constantly reminded by his wife, Edna,
that "everything was gonna be so ducky
. . . a cottage by the waterfall, Roses in
Picardy"; Flor and Ivy, who can't get
married because taxi-driving doesn't pay;
the young actor, Philips, who can't get a
job because producers can't find money
for new plays. Like their creator, they
looked at life and saw "much terror" in
it. Galsworthy saw just such terror in the
inhuman prison system and wrote *Justice*.
Ibsen, earlier, saw the terror in the hypo-
crisy of his society and wrote *Ghosts, A
Doll's House, Pillars of Society, Hedda
Gabler,* and *An Enemy of the People.*

Perhaps Shakespeare saw the "terror"
and concentrated the misery of a large
group into his individual tragic heroes,
his Brutus, Hamlet, Macbeth, Lear, and
Shylock. Perhaps the Greek triumvirate,
Aeschylus, Sophocles, and Euripides, were
actuated by the same feelings when they
created their great trilogies. A survey of
the history of the drama makes quite clear
even to the cursory reader that its leading
figures have almost invariably been moved
by the miseries, the injustices, and the

hypocrisies of life. It was the gift of the artists to cry out boldly, fearlessly, at the risk sometimes of life and limb, at the iniquities visited upon their contemporaries. Every generation must have its Odets to open the eyes of the dull and the sentimental.

And so, it is the theme of frustration which is the motivating force in *Golden Boy*. Poor, cross-eyed Joe Bonaparte— his very name a label that was bound to attract attention! Certainly no Alfred Adler was required to warn us that in the soul of such a man a dreadful inferiority complex was festering that must eventually lead to his tragic end. Joe tried to overcome his handicap with knowledge, by reading Mr. Karp's *Encyclopedia Brittannica;* but in a city where knowledge does not keep people off relief, where doctors drive taxis and lawyers sling hash, the facts of Greek and Roman history and the antics of *Drosophila Melanogaster* would hardly give him peace and freedom. However, one thing Joe did find solace in was music, for then he was not alone. His violin could not call him cock-eyed; Beethoven and Brahms could speak to him and tell him of their own sorrows.

But Joe Bonaparte could not go through life as a cross-eyed violinist. Other human beings were cruel. The next fellow who would make fun of his eyes he would knock down. Fired with this resolve, he studied boxing. Thus began the chain of circumstances that led irresistibly to death in his Dusenberg flattened against a tree.

Joe Bonaparte is indeed the sixth attempt by Odets to dramatize an inferiority complex; for the same type of hero is to be found in all his plays. Soft-spoken actors of the British school could not play an Odets hero, for he cannot be soft-spoken, full of charm and poise. He must yell, must be *gauche*, must scream at his tormentors, must lash out. Odets' large following would seem to be renewed testimony to the fact that most of us are suffering under some sort of inferiority complex; we see in Joe Bonaparte, in Doctor Benjamin, in Ralph Berger of *Awake and Sing*, in Leo Gordon of *Paradise Lost*, in the young revolutionary of *Till the Day I Die*, our own hopes and illusions.

Odets has revealed not only his intentions as a dramatist, but also his methods of writing. His dramatic technique is as important as his theme. In fact, the reviewers were more impressed at first by his technique than by his subject matter.

Odets has revealed the manner in which he developed his skill in giving life to his characters. "I went over my boyhood and tabulated the people's lives which had touched mine," he has said. "I wrote small sketches on yellow paper, and when I read back I saw a strange and wonderful sort of *Spoon River Anthology,* but deeper and more hurting to me because the memories were self-experienced." Odets' characters, therefore, are full of life, easily recognizable. Recall Grandfather Berger, with his music; Pa Berger with his memory of Teddy Roosevelt; Sam Feinshrieber, "the mouse of a man," as his wife calls him; and that grand figure Uncle Morty, whom Franz Hals would have loved to paint. And in Odets' second full-length play there are Gus Michaels, the Irish janitor; and the Gordon family once wealthy but now another depression victim.

His later play *Golden Boy* had the most varied collection of characters of any of his dramas. And the technique is richer. The scene is no longer confined to a single room. Odets has "been around." Eddie Fuseli, the gangster who wants "a piece" of Joe Bonaparte, is as true as Mr. Karp, the disciple of Schopenhauer. What dramatist of our day can create more vivid characters?

Art is not mere imitation of life. Cameras and dictaphones could never create living characters. Though one cannot say he has met a character just like Eddie Fuseli or Mr. Bonaparte, yet one feels that the people on the stage are alive and that somehow we should not forget them for a long time. Odets has created altogether about forty characters, each with a distinct, vibrant personality, an unusual accomplishment for a young playwright.

In 1935, Odets said that he was leaving the Bronx. This he has done not only in a geographical but also a social sense. He has learned the ways of prize-fighters so stupid that they refuse to fight for less than $1,000 and then quarrel with their managers when $1,200 is offered; he has caught the language of the rackets; he has peeped into the heart of an Italian fruit-peddler and there found a love for all mankind. The character of Roxy Gottlieb is a delicious satirical creation. His remark, "If I had hair, I'd tear it out," is so true to his nature that it delights by its appropriateness. Siggie, the taxi-driver, who cannot buy his own cab, whose wife, Anna, fell in love with him when he told her a dirty story the first time he served her in the United Cigar Store—these, too, are living personalities speaking your own language.

Odets' language merits special attention. It is unlike that of any other dramatist in America. Stark Young states, "It seems to me the first thing about Mr. Odets' new play that we should mention is a certain quality in the dialogue . . . The point I wanted to stress as where his theatre gift more appears is in the dialogue's avoidance of the explicit. The explicit, always to be found in poor writers trying to be serious, is the surest sign of lack of talent. To write in terms of what is not said, of combinations elusive and in detail, perhaps, insignificant, of a hidden stream of sequences, and a resulting air of spontaneity and true pleasure —that is quite another matter."

Odets also informs us regarding the origin of this remarkable gift for creating character through dialogue. At the very beginning of his career as a dramatist he learned that, in the words of Galsworthy, "good dialogue is character, marshaled so as continually to stimulate interest or excitement." For characterization Odets has his own very definite theories:

". . . The best procedure, it seems to me, is to take your own subjective experience and self and break that up to bits. I mean to isolate a small portion of one's own personality. When I reminisce I am one character; when I greet my mother after a long absence, another, and so on.

"Objectively and amplifying these facts of one's self makes for sound and organic character. Dostoievsky is a marvellous example of this principle of creative construction. Writers should not cancel their own life experiences, but use them wherever possible.

"I believe sincerely that only when this experience flows into one's work does there begin to be a fighting chance for a writer to become an artist."[3]

But the personal experiences of the playwright, rich as they have been, would not suffice were he not also a master of dramatic construction. Though the number of books on how to write plays grows steadily year after year, their authors do not seem capable themselves of writing the masterpieces which they dangle so temptingly before gullible neophytes (for the requisite tuition fee, of course). Odets, for his part, learned his dramaturgy by studying and acting in plays. For a number of years he acted in stock companies barnstorming up and down the Atlantic coast.

"Although there is little time in stock (he states) to do anything else but learn lines and rehearse, it is possible to absorb a great deal of the playwright's method when it is realized that one plays thirty-two different scripts in one stock season.

"The use of sound theatrical and effective technique seems frowned upon by literary people today. But if we go back to Shakespeare —and who will deny that literary glory?—we come to the greatest creator of sheer theatrical effectiveness in all its aspects. Right now (1935) I'm very busy again with an intensive

[3] *New York Daily Mirror.*

study of his work and begin to realize for the first time what such greatness consists of."

In other respects, too, Shakespeare's practices are followed by Odets. Hamlet makes his own new verb when he uses the expression "to out-Herod Herod." Cleopatra says that she will "un-hair" the courier who brought her news of Antony's marriage to Octavia. Tom Moody says to Lorna Moon, in *Golden Boy*, "Don't Brisbane me" and sets the audience laughing. Odets even creates his own language when necessary. He has Mr. Karp say, "Let me ask you a pertinent remark."

In the light of this brief description of Odets' history, technique, and philosophy of life, we can see more clearly the various stages of his development. In his phenomenal debut-piece, *Waiting for Lefty*, he seemed to have done the inconceivable: he placed a group of men and women on the stage and gave them words. A play resulted. It was unlike any other play the critics had ever seen. One critic called it the greatest one-act play of the century. Perhaps that sounded too much like the advertisement of a boxing-match, but the truth was that the critics were non-plussed. Here was a play that stirred you to your very soul, yet broke all formal laws of construction. Its popularity was unprecedented. The year 1935 saw almost three hundred productions of the play in theatres ranging from South Africa to Seattle. A new talent was heralded.

Awake and Sing opened at the Belasco Theatre on February 19, 1935. It was Odets' first long play, and his sincerity, power of characterization, and "juicy language" (in the words of Percy Hammond) were quickly recognized. It was a study of an unhappy Jewish family in the Bronx. Grandfather Berger had come to America filled with noble dreams and a belief in the realization of Karl Marx's Utopia on our shores. Sadly disappointed, he was now consoled with the thought that his grandson Ralph might help build a better world. Ralph is dissatisfied because he must work so long and so hard that he cannot enjoy the things a young man is entitled to. Moreover, he is in love and wishes to marry, but his mother will not consent to the match. Hennie Berger, her daughter, is an irritable, dissatisfied person, rebelling against the lack of the luxuries which she reads about and sees in the movies. Her position is further aggravated by the fact that she is pregnant as a result of an illicit relationship with the boarder.

Moe Axelrod, her lover, lost a leg in the World War. Bitter against a world which permits wars and resentful because he cannot participate in the pleasures of normal people, he has become sardonic and unscrupulous in his dealings with Hennie.

Mrs. Berger is nervous, imperious, and matriarchial in disposition. Having had the misforture to have married a man without much backbone, she has been the guiding spirit in keeping the family together. Her husband is caught in the inexorable wheels of the depression and seems content with reminiscing of the "Good old days" when Teddy Roosevelt was President.

More vigorous in character is Mrs. Berger's brother Morty, who has built up a successful clothing business. All these characters, to quote Brooks Atkinson, are "excitable, restless and at loose ends; and they are generally flying at one another's throats."

These people are sufficiently interesting to make us forget that the plot is rather thin and that very little happens. When Mrs. Berger discovers that Hennie is to become a mother, she rushes her into marriage with Sam Feinschreiber, whose character is aptly summed up in Hennie's words, "a mouse of a man." Moe Axelrod has no respect for the marriage and persuades Hennie to run off with him to Bermuda. Grandfather Berger, disappointed in his dreams, and having assured himself that his grandson would inherit the proceeds of his life insurance policy, jumps off the roof. The conclusion of the play shows Ralph rushing out from the study with a handful of books. From them he hopes to derive enough knowledge to make a more successful attempt than his grandfather to change the world.

The play was rough in style, it stood still at times, but it stirred its audience more than much better ones. It was the work of a young man writing of the frustrated young men and women all about him. Gilbert Gabriel aptly summed up its theme:

"The youth of the tenements . . . that is Mr. Odets' occupation in this stirring little play. The youth which stubs its fingers on typewriter keys and packing edges all day long and which scuttles to the neighborhood vaudeville and street-corner gangdom by night."

The play was one of many folk-plays of Jewish life, but it appeared to many critics, of whom Richard Lockridge is typical that "of all the many pictures of this *genre*, which has been hung in the theatre's gallery of recent years, this is, in its detail, one of the most convincing and forceful."

Odets avoided the sentimentality which is found in so many folk-plays, of which The Spewack's *Spring Song* was typical.

This sentimentality is a heritage of the Golden Age of the Yiddish theatre of the Bowery days at the beginning of the century. Gordin was turning out plays with amazing rapidity. Jacob P. Adler, father of Luther and Stella who appeared in *Awake and Sing,* was the theatrical idol of the East Side. Audiences enjoyed the stirring of their emotions, even when the melodrama fairly dripped over the stage.

Awake and Sing represented an advance over *Waiting for Lefty,* which revealed the author as a social dramatist, or as Richard Lockridge of the *New York Sun* expressed it, "revolutionary." The first play was written almost immediately after his observation of the unsuccessful taxi-strike in New York in the Spring of 1934. It was pro-labor or "propagandist." It seemed to be lacking in all dramatic technique. *Awake and Sing* was in the tradition of the Russian master Chekhov. John Mason Brown of the *New York Evening Post* declared, "The simple fact remains that of all the American playwrights who have attempted to employ Chekhov's method, none has used it to such advantage as Mr. Odets has in *Awake and Sing.*" Unlike Chekhov's characters who take such a hopeless view of life, however, Hennie and Ralph Berger awake and struggle to find their own salvation.

The play was a kind of hybrid of the spirit of Chekhov and the American Pioneer.

In April, 1935, Odets completed a play about Nazi Germany in five days and offered it together with *Waiting for Lefty*. *Till the Day I Die* was based on a letter from a German writer which had been translated in the *New Masses*. A German communist was arrested while working in the underground movement. After weeks of torture he was released. His comrades had suffered from the treachery of stool-pigeons and were hesitant about giving him work with the movement. He was arrested a second time and tortured physically as well as by the taunts of the nazis that his comrades had no longer any faith in him. When released a second time he unwittingly caused the arrest of all who spoke to him. Finally, he came to his brother and asked him to kill him.

Odets read the English translation and in the heat of anger wrote his seven-scene play in almost record time. Critics were somewhat disappointed because its horror was unconvincing. The author was not familiar enough with the material to give it the verisimilitude which had characterized *Awake and Sing*. For the anti-fascist audience it had the appeal which any attack on nazi brutality would have engendered. It did not indicate any artistic growth and indicated rather that at times Odets' emotions ran away with his artistic principles.

Till the Day I Die was nothing to be ashamed of. Its subject-matter was such as to make almost any play unbelievable. In fact, when other dramatists tried to write about nazi Germany they were also criticized for being too melodramatic. Elmer Rice's *Judgment Day,* Leslie Reed's *The Shatter'd Lamp,* and Friedrich Wolf's *Professor Mamlock* were all criticized as unbelievable, although in each case the dramatist contended that he was merely reporting the facts. In truth, the story of nazi Germany is so horrifying that on the stage it is unbelievable. Odets was handling material which simply refused to be molded into dramatic form.

The dramatist was obviously experimenting with dramatic types, for in April, 1935, he wrote a "progaganda" monologue especially for Morris Carnovsky, who had previously created the character of Grandfather Berger. The speaker has passed up a beggar, who stares at him so pathetically that he must defend himself for not giving anything. As the confession continues, the speaker reveals his miserable existence. Like Grandfather Berger in *Awake and Sing,* he, too, had once been an idealist, but now he had become hard and calloused to all the nobler aspects of existence. He concludes with a condemnation of himself for betraying his early ideals. As an exercise in the monologue of social significance, *I Can't Sleep* was undoubtedly unique.

Paradise Lost, Odets' second full-length drama, opened on December 9, 1935. It was the fourth play of his to be presented in one year: *Awake and Sing, Till the Day I Die,* and *I Can't Sleep* being the other three. It must be admitted that the critics were disappointed. Gilbert Gabriel, whose praise for the earlier plays was unstinted, regretted that:

". . . Everything that Father Time and his mean lieutenants, the drama critics, ever feared would happen to the talents of Odets has evidently been happening now. Everything that would reduce the fiery attractiveness of an *Awake and Sing* to fog, almost to foolishness, has turned up in exaggerated quantity in *Paradise Lost* and made of it a grotesque with a dozen oratorical arms and not a leg to stand on."

Odets left no doubt as to his intentions, for he sent out an announcement prior to the performance that the hero in *Paradise Lost* was the entire American middle class of liberal tendency. The Gordon family was represented as living somewhere in the East. This time they were not definitely Jewish like the Bergers of *Awake and Sing.* Mr. Gordon had manufactured ladies' pocketbooks until the depression killed the demand for them. One of his sons is slowly dying from encaphalitis; another had been a famous runner until he had developed a bad heart. The daughter is a pianist who cannot marry the man she loves because he has no job. Other characters introduced are the garrulous Gus Michaels, a family friend; Marcus Katz, the unscrupulous partner who suggests that they burn their factory and collect insurance with which to start a new business; Mr. May, a professional incendiary who has arson down to a science; Mr. Pike, a pacifist furnace man; and various other typical members of American society.

The criticism of the play was unfavorable. Though the reviewers were willing to accept the Berger family as an authentic representation of Bronx Jewry, the Gordons were not convincing. As Robert Garland wrote, "They aren't American, they aren't middle-class, they aren't alive." Richard Lockridge, dramatic critic of the *New York Sun,* was more explicit in his disapproval.

"If it were less realistically described, one might suspect the author of symbolism. As realism it is ridiculous, comic exaggeration. A a charter member of the American middle class of liberal tendency I assure Mr. Odets that it is not in the least like this; that what he has achieved is a mixture of shrill melodrama and caricature and that his religious faith in the revolution is descending like a curtain between him and the people of the real world, whom it is every dramatist's duty to observe."

Odets was not content to accept the derogatory criticisms without challenging their validity. "*Paradise Lost* is my best and most mature play," he said. "By far! And without reservation." Since most of the critics had commented on the Chekhovian echoes in the play, Odets felt it necessary to explain that "Chekhov was mentioned in that statement (released to the press before the première) as historic reference, not to point out his influence on my work,—one which, incidentally, is still doubtful in my own mind. You have my word for it that I intend to read *The Cherry Orchard* tonight for the first time in my life."

Because so much skepticism had been expressed about the verisimilitude of his portrait of the American middle class, Odets attempted to defend his characterization.

"Some of us are inclined to think today that we are surrounded on all sides by normal, well-juiced people (he said). We are apt to forget that day by day millions of intellectuals, professionals, and white-collar workers are gently being eased out of comforts they once knew, surely being declassed and dispossessed. Perhaps many of us living in comfort, well-cushioned away from reality, know little of what is going on. Little or nothing.

"Perhaps these comfortable, well-cushioned ones, able to buy drinks at Tony's or 21—surely full of sane, normal people, as John O'Hara has brilliantly shown—are not aware that twenty-eight million Americans are living on relief of various kinds. Perhaps we have not seen the delicate psychological manifestations of their degradation."

Perhaps the disappointment of the critics was due to their expectations, which only a master-dramatist could have fulfilled. It is embarrassing to be called the "white hope of the American theatre" before one's thirtieth birthday. The gifts of dramatic dialogue, vivid characterization, and theatrical sense may be granted to a young man, but the greater gift of understanding the decline of a great class comes only with age and maturity. Odets did not know enough of the American middle class whose demoralization he tried so earnestly to depict. Besides, any drama in which a "class" is a hero is bound to cause confusion. To emphasize the afflictions of his representative American family, he piled calamity upon calamity which had no connection with his economic thesis. There was no reason for introducing the slowly dying Julie, since his lingering illness might have occurred in Biblical, feudal or renaissance times. Here and there, slightly overcome by the temptation to show his skill at revealing the varied elements that constitute character, Odets introduced asides and monologues which were irrelevant to his theme and plot.

The play aroused considerable discussion, which was one indication of its vitality. It was by no means a failure. Rather was it not the masterpiece his admirers were led to expect. For two years he did not produce another drama. He had received a call to Hollywood whither Franchot Tone and J. Edward Bromberg, fellow-members of the Group Theatre, had gone earlier. One of his pictures, *The General Died at Dawn,* was marked by a few speeches which revealed the social viewpoint of its author. Odets was not inactive in his playwriting. Rumors came to Broadway that he was writing a play about the prize-ring and one about business. *Golden Boy,* produced in November, 1937, is the first. It is generally assumed that *Golden Boy* is his most important play to date and that Hollywood did not have the deteriorating effect which it usually has upon the gifted young dramatists lured there by high salaries. If anything, Odets has become keener in his perception of men and women, more precise in his dramatic idiom, and more aware of the intricacies of human nature.

Golden Boy is the story of the rise and fall of a cross-eyed, sensitive Italian boy who becomes a successful pugilist and finally dies in an automobile crash after his most successful fight. In telling this story Odets introduces the machinery of fight promotion, racketeering in the boxing game, and the family life of the Bonapartes, hard-working, simple, kindly Italians. The "collapse of the American middle-class" which was pictured in *Paradise Lost* has given way to the study of the making of an individual, in the manner of Shakespeare, rather than Chekhov. Not that Odets has lost his awareness of the class struggle. Joe Bonaparte's brother is a C.I.O. organizer, who is working among the Southern textile laborers. Mr. Karp is a favorite character with Odets—the commentator on the sadness of the *status quo*. In *Awake and Sing* it was Grandfather Berger; in *Paradise Lost* it was Gus Michaels. Siggie's inability to buy a taxi so that he can be independent of the "bosses" is another indication of Odets' interest in the difficulties of the working class.

The superiority of *Golden Boy* to the other dramas is apparent in the diversity of characters, in the coherence of his plot, and in the omission of the non-essential elements which cluttered up the earlier dramas. While in his experimental stage, in the heat of his emotions, Odets was inclined to permit speeches which were good economics but bad dramatic dialogue. In his later play the dialogue proceeds inevitably from the characters and the plot proceeds from the dialogue in a manner that would have warmed the heart of John Galsworthy.

Rocket to the Moon dealt with the drab existence of a dentist who was still hopeful of some of the beauty and romance in life. It had little of the social significance which distinguished the other plays.

Night Music had the shortest run of any play by Odets, yet to his many admirers it represented the fruition of his talents. It deals with the insecurity of contemporary youth. In its bare outlines it is a boy-meets-girl story, yet it represents the tragic futility and hopelessness of our times as few plays have succeeded in doing. Perhaps the presence of Elmer Rice's *Two on an Island* at the same time removed a potential audience for Odets' play.

In summing up Odets' qualities as a writer of drama, one can distinguish several outstanding virtues. First, he is concrete, dramatizing in vivid terms the ideas and acts of his characters. Secondly, he has used his knowledge and love for music to give his dramas a symphonic quality which naturally enriches them. Life is not a matter of a simple melody, and in telling of the rise and fall of one person, one would be untrue to life to omit the strands of minor plots of other persons in the play. Odets has always brought in several life-stories in his dramas. In *Waiting for Lefty* about a dozen victims of the depression were analyzed. In his larger dramas he has always tried by skillful exposition to present the past of each character, sometimes too generously. In *Golden Boy*, all these themes are combined into a dramatic symphony, with a skill found in few dramatists writing today.

Thirdly, his dialogue is pungent, revelatory of character, memorable for its quotability, devoid of any unnecessary elements, and charged with dramatic intensity. Even when the critics were disappointed with the confused thinking of *Paradise Lost,* they still admired the brilliant dialogue. It may lack the poetry of which Maxwell Anderson is the master; it has not the characteristic recognizability of Elmer Rice's language in *Street Scene;* nor has it George S. Kaufman's gaglike smartness. It has, however, force and inevitability.

Finally, Odets aims to write plays of social significance and interpretation. He is following in the footsteps of Ibsen, of the early Hauptmann, of Shaw, and of their numerous imitators. Perhaps he expresses best his philosophy of playwriting in his own words, written after the première of *Golden Boy*.

It is about time that the talented American playwright began to take the gallery of American types, the assortment of fine vital themes away from the movies. This was attempted in *Golden Boy*. Some critics were surprised at the choice of theme. Where is there a more interesting theme in this country than a little Italian boy who wants to be rich? Provided, of course, you place him in his true social background and show his fellow conspirators in their true light, bring out the essential loneliness and bewilderment of the average citizen, do not blow trumpets for all that is corrupt and wicked around the little Italian boy, do not substitute a string of gags for reality of experience, present the genuine pain, meaning and dignity of life within your characters.

As spokesman for the Americans who are not found in the 4% tail which wags the 96% dog, for the Americans who are not mentioned in Lundberg's *Sixty Families*, but of the Americans who sought in our cities and on our plains a land where human liberty would be a reality, where human labor would earn its just reward, and where human dignity would be cherished, regardless of creed or race, Clifford Odets deserves the laureateship.

PART TWO

PLAYS

Two Decades of Biographical Plays

AMERICAN audiences like Abraham Lincoln but are indifferent to Napoleon. They have listened to Victoria Regina for three years, but only one week is granted to Marie Antoinette. They fall in love with Elizabeth Barrett, but care little for Jane Austen, Emily Dickinson, or the Bronte sisters. The lives of Poe, Keats, and Shelley are less interesting than the extravagances of Oscar Wilde. Jesse James is more real than Arnold Rothstein. Richard Wagner, Gaudier-Brzeska and Sir Arthur Sullivan are less significant than Schubert and Pieter Stuyvesant. How can these tastes and preferences be explained? Why does one biographical play take Broadway by storm while a dozen others similar in style and content close after brief runs? These are some of the questions which the observer of the contemporary American drama would like to answer.

Dramatists and producers, recalling the extraordinary success of the Victorian love story of the Barretts in New York and its equally encouraging reception on tour, are always hoping that there's still gold in the Dictionary of National Biography or in the Encyclopedia Americana.

Since packed houses greeted Katherine Cornell night after night as Elizabeth Barrett, why should not the same reception be given to Helen Gahagan as Emily Bronte, Linda Watkins as Miss Godwin, Eva Le Gallienne as L'Aiglon, or Dorothy Gish as Emily Dickinson? It is a logical question, but in the theatre, logic has rarely determined the success or failure of any production.

Hardly a dramatic season goes by without several new biographical plays. Boom years, Depression years, New Deal years and War years have all seen princes and poets, kings, queens, courtesans, and scientists strut about and fret their usually brief hours upon the stage to be heard no more. Critics write glibly and copiously on the esthetics and dramaturgics of this type of play. No sooner does one expire when almost all of the reviewers seize the opportunity for a literary post-mortem to explain to a usually uninterested audience why Keats, Shelley or Poe was dull on the stage.

Biographical plays appear on the average of five each season. Perhaps it will be most illuminating for this discussion to list the characters studied for a few seasons and draw certain conclusions from them. New York audiences have seen the following named personalities on the stage:

Two Decades of Biographical Plays

LIVING CHARACTERS	NAME OF PLAY	AUTHOR	NO. OF PER-FORMANCES
Season of 1928-1929			
Irving Berlin	*The Song Writer*	Crane Wilbur	56
Chopin	*White Lilacs* (musical)	Sigurd Johannsen	136
Faust	*Faust*	Goethe	48
Macchiavelli	*The Grey Fox*	Lemist Esler	88
Sacco and Vanzetti	*Gods of the Lightning*	Maxwell Anderson and Harold Hickerson	29
Edmund Kean	*The Royal Box*	Alexandre Dumas	39
Cyrano de Bergerac	*Cyrano de Bergerac*	Edmund Rostand	143
Falstaff	*Falstaff*	James Plaisted Webber	15
Richelieu	*The Red Robe*	Stanley Weyman	167
Judas	*Judas*	Walter Ferris	7
Alexander the Great	*Young Alexander*	Hardwick Nevin	7

95

Two Decades of Biographical Plays

LIVING CHARACTERS	NAME OF PLAY	AUTHOR	NO. OF PER-FORMANCES
	Season of 1929-1930		
Isidora Duncan	Diana	Irving K. Davis	8
Richelieu	Richelieu	Edward Bulwer-Lytton	86
Arnold Rothstein	Room 349	Mark Linder	15
	Season of 1930-1931		
Emily Dickinson	Alison's House	Susan Glaspell	42
Elizabeth and Robert Browning	The Barretts of Wimpole Street	Rudolf Besier	372
Aaron Burr	Colonel Satan	Booth Tarkington	17
Queen Elizabeth	Elizabeth the Queen	Maxwell Anderson	145
Empress Josephine	Napi	Julius Berstl	21
Tom Mooney	Precedent	I. J. Golden	184
Cesare Borgia	The Tyrant	Raphael Sabatini	13

97

Two Decades of Biographical Plays

LIVING CHARACTERS	NAME OF PLAY	AUTHOR	NO. OF PER- FORMANCES
Charles II and friends	*The Love of Charles II*	Cornelia Otis Skinner	22
Chatterton	*Come of Age*	Clemence Dane	35
John Brown	*John Brown*	Ronald Gow	2
Theodora	*Theodora the Queen*	Jo Milward	
		J. Kerbey Hawkes	6
Richard II	*Richard of Bordeaux*	Gordon Daviot	39
Scottsboro Defendants	*Legal Murder*		7
Scottsboro Defendants	*They Shall Not Die*	John Wexley	62
Catiline, Cicero	*When in Rome*	Austin Major	7
Walter Reed	*Yellow Jack*	Sidney Howard	79
Brontës	*Moor Born*	Dan Totheroh	63

Season of 1934-1935

Hitler, Goering	*Judgment Day*	Elmer Rice	94

Character	Play	Author	
Duke of Reichstadt	*L'Aiglon*	Edmund Rostand	58
Emily Dickinson	*Brittle Heaven*	Vincent York and Frederick J. Pohl	23
George Washington	*Valley Forge*	Maxwell Anderson	58
Richelieu	*Richelieu*	Edward Bulwer-Lytton	10
Noah	*Noah*	Andre Obey	46
Biblical Characters	*The Green Pastures*	Marc Connelly	1000+
Johann Strauss, Sr. and Jr.	*The Great Waltz*	Moss Hart	297

Season of 1935-1936

Character	Play	Author	
Parnell	*Parnell*	Elsie Schauffler	98
Victoria	*Victoria Regina*	Laurence Housman	515
Joan of Arc	*Saint Joan*	Bernard Shaw	88
George V	*Jubilee*	Moss Hart	169
Sacco	*Winterset*	Maxwell Anderson	194

Season of 1936-1937

Character	Play	Author	
Franz Joseph	*White Horse Inn*	Hans Mueller	211
Napoleon	*St. Helena*	R. C. Sheriff and Jeanne de Casalis	63

Two Decades of Biographical Plays

LIVING CHARACTERS	NAME OF PLAY	AUTHOR	NO. OF PER-FORMANCES
Henri Gaudier and Sophie Brzeska	*The Laughing Woman*	Gordon Daviot	23
Edgar Allen Poe	*Plumes in the Dust*	Sophie Treadwell	11
Richard Wagner	*Prelude to Exile*	William McNally	48
John Keats	*Aged 26*	Anne Crawford Flexner	32
Biblical Characters	*The Eternal Road*	Franz Werfel	152
Franz Joseph, Rudolph	*The Masque of Kings*	Maxwell Anderson	89
Benedict Arnold	*A Point of Honor*	Jo Elsinger Stephen Von Gluck	5
Eleonora Duse	*Curtain Call*	Le Roy Bailey	4
John Barrymore and Elaine Barrie	*Hitch Your Wagon*	Bernard C. Schoenfeld	28

101

102

Thus we see that about 100 biographical plays were produced in the years 1928-1947. The distribution of characters is interesting.

Musicians (8): Irving Berlin, Chopin, Johann Strauss, Richard Wagner, Sir Arthur Sullivan, Gus Edwards, Edward Grieg, Johann Strauss, Jr.

Writers (19): Faust, Cyrano de Bergerac, Emily Dickinson, Elizabeth and Robert Browning, Boccaccio, Bernard Shaw, Luigi Pirandello, Shakespeare, Chatterton, Brontë Sisters, Edgar Allen Poe, John Keats, Percy B. Shelley, Richard Steele, W. S. Gilbert, Oscar Wilde, Charles Dickens, Harriet Beecher Stowe.

Political Leaders (36): Macchiavelli, Richelieu, Alexander, Aaron Burr, Queen Elizabeth, Empress Josephine, Cesare Borgia, Abraham Lincoln (5), Napoleon (2), Mary, Queen of Scots, Charles II, John Brown, Theodora, Richard II, Catiline, Cicero, Hitler, Goering, Duke of Reichstadt, George Washington (2), Parnell, Queen Victoria, Joan of Arc, George V, Franz Joseph of Austria (3), Benedict Arnold, Toussaint L'Ouverture, Cleopatra, Antony, Franklin D. Roosevelt, Julius Caesar, Governor of Virginia, Disraeli,

Pieter Stuyvesant, Marie Antoinette, Kosciusko, Anne of England, Catherine the Great, Henry VIII, Joan of Arc.

Actors (6): Jeanne Eagles, Eleanora Duse, John Barrymore, Elaine Barrie, Kean, John Wilkes Booth.

Scientist (1): Walter Reed.

Artist (2): Henri Gaudier, Benvenuto Cellini.

Bon Vivant (1): Falstaff.

Religious Characters (2): Judas, Noah.

Dancer (1): Isidora Duncan.

Explorer (1): Columbus.

Prisoners or Criminals (6): Arnold Rothstein, Tom Mooney, Scottsboro Boys (2), Sacco, Vanzetti (2), Jesse James.

Nurse (1): Florence Nightingale.

Judge (1): O. W. Holmes.

Miscellaneous: The Dubarry, Lucrece, Annie Oakley, Mary Surratt.

Political leaders and authors make the most popular subjects for biographical dramas. Why are some of these plays more successful than others? *Victoria Regina* and *The Barretts of Wimpole Street* are perhaps the most popular biographical dramas in recent years. Is the writing, the acting, or the personality the determining factor in making one play a hit and another a failure? Do biographical plays come in cycles? These are some of the questions for which answers will be welcomed. In this study an attempt will be made to supply some adequate basis for discussion and critical evaluation of the biographical drama.

A glance at the history of this form of dramatic art will be useful. The most obvious contrast between the biographical dramas of our time and those of the ancient classical dramatists or the French or German classical authors is the humbler station of the characters portrayed. Schiller might write of Wallenstein or even William Tell, but he would certainly not devote a play to the life, however fascinating it may have been, of a painter or an author. Goethe in his *Egmont* and his *Goetz* delineated historically important figures. Even though Voltaire discussed the Jean Calas scandal in a pamphlet, it would have been inconceivable to write a play about him as John Wexley wrote of the Scottsboro Negroes or as Maxwell Anderson wrote of Sacco and Vanzetti. All of this might easily be explained by the spread of democracy and a consequent elevation of the importance of the accomplishments of those who were not kings or conquerors. As a matter of fact the sufferings from the threat of a tyrannical father and her eventual revolt have made Elizabeth Barrett a far more believable person than the machinations of a dozen rulers and their wives or mistresses.

The heroic is no longer confined to military or political victories. A scientist discovering the carrier of the germ of yellow fever is to the audiences of today more engrossing than Napoleon, Richelieu, Cesare Borgia or Macchiavelli. Dramatists have not been unaware of the growing interest in the heroic element in our daily lives, and have presented a gallery of dramatic portraits that includes the sacrifices of Florence Nightingale, the courage of Tom Mooney, Sacco and Vanzetti, and the Scottsboro Negroes.

Certain political leaders seem to interest dramatists and audiences more than others. Including John Drinkwater's *Abraham Lincoln* (1919), five plays have appeared about the Great Emancipator within the last two decades. Only two plays were written about George Washington, one each about Aaron Burr, Benedict Arnold, John Brown, and Pieter Stuyvesant. The "dramatizability" of Abraham Lincoln is explained in many ways: his truly American rise from log cabin to White House, his human qualities, his historical importance as the Emancipator, and his humor.

Why are plays about Honest Abe so

successful? John Drinkwater's drama described him as President. Goodman's *If Booth Had Missed* presented a post-bellum picture. E. P. Conkle's *Prologue to Glory* concerns an awkward, hesitant youth in his twenties. Robert E. Sherwood's *Abe Lincoln in Illinois* is more episodic than the others, covering a period of over thirty years in his life. Sherwood's own statements concerning his decision to dramatize Lincoln's life offer a rare opportunity to the student of a dramatist's methods and predilections.

"I don't remember when I first mentioned it (the idea of writing a play on Lincoln) . . ." he told an interviewer of the *New York World-Telegram. The Prairie Years* by Carl Sandburg awakened Mr. Sherwood's interest in the strange emotionalism of Lincoln as a young man.

"Up to then," Mr. Sherwood said, "I'd thought that he was a statue, even while he was living. I thought he certainly was the embodiment of all that was noble and courageous and heroic."

After reading considerable material on Lincoln's life—speeches, letters, and memoirs of contemporaries, Sherwood found that "this wasn't a job of playwriting. It was a job of editing. After

I got my material together, it was just a good job of carpentering."

It is safe to say that Lincoln as a doubting, frustrated, self-conscious human being has had more appeal than Lincoln the President. One of the most dramatic scenes in Sherwood's play is the moment before the arrival of three politicians who want to look the prospective candidate over. All the bickerings and humiliations which Lincoln had to endure his married life through from the ever-sharp and ever-moving tongue of Mary Todd are concentrated in a few moments of superb dramatic writing. The tragedy of Lincoln as an unhappy man was more pitiful than the tragedy of Lincoln as the victim of a crazed actor.

It is the dramatic quality in the everyday life of famous personalities which has made plays about them popular. Thus Elizabeth Barrett's drinking of the port wine much against her will, and her struggle to raise herself from her couch in order to catch a last glimpse of Robert Browning as he leaves her after his first visit are ineffably more moving than all the pseudo-dramatic wrestlings with words and plaster and melodies of which so many plays about artists consist. This observation seems fairly true. Audiences de-

sire in a biographical drama of an artist,
not details of their artistic creations, but
accounts of happenings in their daily lives.
Even in artists the spectators have asked
to be shown the human being. When William McNally in *Prelude to Exile* devoted
almost an entire act to Wagner's amorous
protestations to Matilda von Wesendonck
prior to his sudden hearing of the love-
theme of *Tristan*, he failed to interest his
audiences. Poe's struggles with metaphors
and rhymes, Shelley's recitations before
Godwin, Emily Dickinson's and Jane Austen's surreptitious scribblings were of little
consequence. Dramatists have not learned,
from the repeated failures of so many
plays about literary people, that literary
creation is hardly dramatic, that the in-
diting of a sonnet is not an act to hold a
thousand spectators breathless with excitement, that the playing of the theme of
a song will not satisfy drama-hungry men
and women. The sooner playwrights
realize that artists are human beings and
that only as human beings can they arouse
any empathic reactions, the fewer failures
will there be in biographical dramas.

Next to the democracy in subject-matter
and the interest in the human-natural elements in the lives of famous folk, the third
characteristic of the contemporary successful biographical drama is simplicity of

language. Abe Lincoln's comment on the two "d"s in Mary Todd as a sign of her conceit inasmuch as there was only one "d" in God; Victoria's request for a room of her own in the first scene of Housman's play; Robert Browning's exclamation of dismay at his inability to understand a passage of *Sordello,* saying that only "God knew what it meant, whereas in the writing both God and he knew"—these comparatively simple touches take on a dramatic incandescence which seems to illuminate the character long after other apparently more important scenes are forgotten. Violent deaths, flamboyant oratory, incendiary revolts on the part of poets or painters do not seem as compelling behind the footlights as a few simple words of tenderness or passion uttered slowly and quietly. When Poe struggled with *delirium tremens* on the hospital bed, in Sophie Treadwell's *Plumes in the Dust,* he did not arouse sympathy but a slight feeling of revulsion. When Young Disraeli or Shelley ranted against intolerant politicians or ignorant, conventional reviewers, somehow these violent outbursts left one cold. Yet Parnell's reticent lovemaking and Lincoln's prayer for a sick boy made long-lasting impressions. Literary or artistic language in a play about literary or artistic people is rarely of interest to an audience since it is most often composed of non-creative individuals. Emily Dickinson's speech in *Brittle Heaven* was studded with gems which were taken from her own poems, yet the play did not succeed. When Robert Sherwood quotes entire paragraphs from Lincoln's addresses, as he does in the famous Lincoln-Douglas debate scene, he is fortunate in having a speech whose simple effectiveness is now proverbial. There is no "fancy" language anywhere in the play, although at times it may seem old-fashioned in its conventionality. The simplicity of Lincoln's language in Sherwood's play is found also in E. P. Conkle's *Prologue to Glory* and Drinkwater's *Abraham Lincoln*. It contrasts so strongly with the bombast of the neurotic Duke of Raichstadt, for example, or the violent invectives of Disraeli.

It will be instructive, at this point, to study each group of biographies for the purpose of generalizing about the present tendencies of dramatists and audiences. Apparently the dramatization of musicians' lives can best be done by incorporating their music into the plays. The life of Wagner was a failure even though several famous melodies were introduced as integral elements of the play. The portrait of the composer as a heartless egotist, oblivious of any duty to wife, mistress or friend was too unpalatable. Such a revelation does not help us to understand the genius who composed the *Ring*. Nor was his life heroic enough to inspire worship. Carlyle said that hero-worship was a fundamental instinct of the human mind. Clayton Hamilton, elaborating the idea, continues:

"Nothing else so strongly stirs emotion in a multitude as the visible presence of a hero, whatever be the nature of his prowess."

Yet, the life of Wagner, troublesome as it was, could not by any stretch of the imagination be called heroic. It is better to know nothing about the origin of the Love-Potion music of *Tristan* than to see the protestations of a married man to the wife of his dear friend result in the inspiration which eventually became the beloved theme.

The musical versions of the lives of Schubert in *Blossom Time,* Chopin in *White Lilacs,* and the Strausses in *The Great Waltz* were far more successful. Granted that there was more romantic glamor attached to the composers than to Wagner. Yet, the dramatists made no pretense at presenting biographies. Romantic idealizations might best describe these treatments. Musical composition *per se* can be of little dramatic value. The picture of a great composer making black marks on sheets of ruled paper is of no dramatic power. Thus the musicalizations made up in colorful costumes and settings and the undying music for the lack of real dramatic material. The life of Sir Arthur Sullivan was a complete failure on the stage although his operettas have always found a sympathetic response. Generalizing about the biographical treatments of musicians, one can conclude that only the music of the subject and the romantic idealization of a few experiences make a success on the stage.

When we study the plays about authors we have more material at hand. Keats, Shelley, and Chatterton had short lives on the New York stage. With Shelley was presented that entire strange and fascinating Godwin family. The characters all seemed believable and the picture seemed historically correct in costuming and settings. Yet this play, which to English audiences might have had a more intimate appeal, failed to make much of an impression. In searching for an explanation of the coldness of American audiences to the vicissitudes in the lives of great English poets, somehow, one cannot escape the feeling that our own problems are too overpowering to make many people interested in the personal difficulties of poets of another land a hundred years ago. One hesitates to mix economics and aesthetics, yet, how can audiences who read of wars and mass starvation find much to interest them in Shelley's search for funds to publish his poems? The fact is that the problems of these poets are so personal and so unimportant to anyone except the poet, that a large theatre audience cannot find enough in the play to warrant spending an evening with it.

Everyone who goes to the theatre can understand and appreciate emotions which made the characters of *The Barretts of Wimpole Street* so believable. There was something of the problem of *Romeo and Juliet* in it. The clashes of parents and children have always made good dramatic timber. The occupation of poetry-writing was only incidental to the more understandable occupation of living one's own life and loving.

Dramatists of biographical plays have made the fatal mistake of believing that theatre-goers would take the trouble to leave their homes, endure the inconveniences of travelling to the theatre, in order to see a series of scenes of the life of a well-known poet presented behind the footlights. When such a biography of Poe exists as Hervey Allen's *Israfel,* why should an audience spend an evening in the theatre with Sophie Treadwell's *Plumes in the Dust?* The answer is that audiences refused after six evenings to have anything to do with Poe, so long as they could still read his stories and poems at home. The spectacle of a poet reciting his own poems is hardly inspiring. This particular study of Poe was melodramatic rather than dramatic, confusing rather than revelatory. Artistic creation is too subtle and evanescent to be capable of convincing dramatization. Source-hunting had better be left to the scholars rather than to the dramatists. Unless the experiences of the artist as a human being are capable of striking responsive chords of sympathetic understanding, the dramatist had better desist from delineating such characters.

The success of Besier's play about Elizabeth Barrett must have raised the hopes of dramatists of the lives of other feminine authors. Yet, Vincent York and Frederick Pohl's study of Emily Dickinson (*Brittle Heaven*) and Dan Totheroh's *Moor Born* Brontes could not repeat the success of the earlier play. It must be admitted that the life of the "Nun of Amherst" was not very exciting and that her one love affair was hardly capable of stirring an audience. Frailty and delicacy of expression may be quite acceptable when the character is discussed in a book, but on the stage they leave one cold and unmoved. Perhaps the troubles of the times have something to do with an audience's reactions to biographical plays. The response to *Abe Lincoln* is so sincere because his problems are so similar to our own. Most people in the average audience feel a bond of sympathy with an awkward, unhandsome, uncertain lad who was tortured throughout his life by doubts and fears; who lost the two women he really loved, his mother and Ann Rutledge; who rarely found happiness in his home or in public office; and whose sadness was the sadness of the human race. Few audiences, however, can force themselves to sympathize with a sorrow that is peculiar to the poet as was Emily Dickinson's. The play then becomes a mere literary curiosity and as such loses its effectiveness as a stimulus to the emotions. It is understandable how a dramatist deeply interested in the works of a poet or novelist, making a special study of him, eventually becomes so enthralled with his life that the poet is more important than his works. He then proceeds to write a play about Shelley or Keats or Jane Austen. On it he lavishes all his knowledge of their lives, all his rich recollection of their speech, and endeav-

ors to build it all around one big love
affair. The theatre-audience, however,
fails to see anything important in all this.
A writer's works may be immortal yet his
life on the stage may be insufferably dull.
Besides, there is the sad confession that
the hundreds of thousands of spectators
who are necessary to make a play successful are usually not the poetry-reading
kind. Emily Dickinson's life ran for
twenty-three performances, which probably exhausted the number of those who
ever heard of her or read her poetry. One
did not even have to know a line of Elizabeth Barrett's poetry to be enchanted by
Besier's play.

The drama is a popular art-form, relying upon the support of hundreds of
thousands if successes are to result. One's
illusions should not prevent the realization
that the poetry in a poet's life does not
mean much to a metropolis where five
million people each Sunday read one tab-
loid newspaper.

As would be expected, most of the biographical dramas concern political figures.
Among the Americans we find Pieter Stuyvesant, George Washington, Aaron Burr,
Benedict Arnold, John Brown, Abraham
Lincoln, and Franklin D. Roosevelt. In no
other country could its ruler be treated as

was our President in *I'd Rather Be Right*.

The play is probably the first of its kind to mention a nation's leader and speak lightly of easily recognizable traits. In England the law forbiding the representation of living members of the royal family prevents either humorous or serious portrayals of leaders of the state. This law caused much difficulty when attempts were made to produce Laurence Housman's *Victoria Regina* in London. Although no objection was offered to its performance in a small, privately endowed theatre, permission to move the play to a larger house open to the public was withheld. There was observed the strange phenomenon, consequently, of a play about England's great Queen of the nineteenth century winning unprecedented success in America, yet being denied to English playgoers because one of the characters represented as a child was the former Queen ·of Spain. Perhaps the height of irony was reached when the former Queen saw the performance in New York and expressed her satisfaction with both the play and the exquisite performance of Helen Hayes.

It is interesting to compare the treatment of national heroes in the drama of different countries. In American drama, it is safe to say chauvinism is hardly apparent. On the other hand a drama about Napoleon in French is inconceivable except as a glorification. Even *L'Aiglon,* which Rostand conceived as an opportunity for Coquelin to play a grumpy greadier *"a grandes moustaches,"* turned out a tribute to the Corsican, although the time of the play had been advanced to 1830 and only his weakling son appeared on the stage. But, contrary to the author's expectation, the dead Napoleon still appealed so emphatically to the public through the person of the ineffective little boy whom he had left behind him, that the part of the Duc de Raichstadt took the play away from the part of Flambeau, and *L'Aiglon,* intended as a vehicle for Coquelin, became instead a vehicle for Sarah Bernhardt.

The Founding Fathers were aware of the power of sane criticism and provided for it in the Constitution by the system of checks and balances. Hence, they would not have objected to the treatment of Washington and his contemporaries in Maxwell Anderson's *Valley Forge.* Nor could they see anything to criticize in the fact that the part of the Father of our country was played by Richard Merivale, a British actor, and that the part of Lincoln in Sherwood's *Abe Lincoln in Illinois* was played by Raymond Massey, a Canadian. Can anyone conceive of the possibility of an American playing Napoleon in Paris or the Duke of Wellington in London?

It is not implied that the dramatists of American heroes are irreverent because they are not idolatrous. On the contrary. They have a great love and admiration for their heroes; else why write a play about them? Instead of giving them legendary treatments, American dramatists have made them men of flesh and blood, subject to the same frailties and passions as the rest of mankind. Thus in *Valley Forge,* Anderson did not hesitate to introduce American pseudo-patriots who were willing to "sell out" the Revolution because they were losing too much in trade by the war. One of the most humorous and yet socially significant scenes of the play occurs when several of these worthy gentlemen visit Washington's headquarters to examine the situation. They had heard of wastes in food. A few samples of the indigestible rations to which even the officers had been reduced were enough to teach these well-fed pillars of society that fighting a war was a bit more inconvenient than financing it.

Anderson's disrespect for some of the early Americans because of their knavery and financial unscrupulousness is evident in his later play *Knickerbocker Holiday* (1938) which concerns Pieter Stuyvesant and his Little New Americans. A more inane and corrupt body of town councillors has rarely appeared before in literature. They admit every crime from traffic with Indians to making a huge profit from selling them arms and liquor. Pieter Stuyvesant is the greatest rogue of them all, being a combination of Il Duce and Realmsleader rolled into one. It is true that in an Epilogue the author begs pardon for any pained feelings he may have caused any of the descendants of the estimable gentlemen mentioned. Even the name of Roosevelt does not escape, and it is this Dutch Roosevelt who leads the revolt against Stuyvesant by refusing to hang the one young man in the colony who will not be bullied by the Governor. "When I get an idea it sticks," says Roosevelt when he has once made up his mind not to pull the hanging-rope. This was only one of the several remarks which the audience interpreted as applicable to our own times as it was three hundred years ago. Anderson's remarks about the susceptibility of democracy to corruption and malfeasance in office were echoes of similar opinions expressed in his Pulitizer Prize Winner of 1931, *Both Your Houses,* and *Valley Forge.* His contempt for intolerance and bloodshed had been heard earlier in *The Wingless Victory* (1936) and *The Masque of Kings* (1937). His hatred for the grossly material and the commercial aspects of life was observed in *High Tor* (1936) and *The Star-Wagon* (1937). Anderson is no hero-worshipper, although he respects the virtues.

The dramatic portraits of other Americans—Aaron Burr, Benedict Arnold, and John Brown are also influenced by the "new" biography which aims to present the man rather than to create an impossible legend. The attempt to justify the treachery of Benedict Arnold as an act of self-sacrifice won little popular support. The American public from its school-days has been brought up on the shame of Arnold's deed. A play, and not a good play at that, could not hope to change such a view overnight. In a volume or series of volumes which one can read leisurely and study carefully it is possible to present an array of new facts which might change the historical significance of any misunderstood character. In the brief period of a play, when facts for facts' sake are taboo, when no opportunity is granted for offering footnotes and contending points of view, the attempt to change a traditional opinion is doomed from the start to fail. Even when a dramatist supplies line and page, on the program, as sources for his scenes, as Sidney Kingsley did with *Ten Million Ghosts* (1936), the audiences could not be moved by historical data which could more readily have been obtained in any library. *John Brown* failed because of inferior treatment by the dramatist.

Several Queens have attracted the attention of playwrights in the past decade: Theodora, Mary of Scots, Elizabeth, Empress Josephine, Victoria, and Marie Antoinette. Maxwell Anderson's *Elizabeth the Queen* and *Mary of Scotland* were popular successes and have won an enviable position in the English curricula of many secondary schools. They have their purple passages in his own variety of blank verse which have helped to make dramatic verse once more a vehicle for nobility of manner as well as thought. Both plays were tragedies, in the one case for Essex and his unfortunate sovereign; in the other for Mary, imprisoned by her British cousin. Relying on easily understandable emotions of love and jealousy, Anderson avoided the bombast and unconvincing artificiality of so many plays of historical figures. Elizabeth may have been every inch a queen in real life, but in the play she was more of a woman, old, vain, unsure of her ability to hold the affections of the man she loved, jealous of his popular favor, and finally afraid of her throne. Anderson's play came shortly after Lytton Strachey's *Elizabeth and Essex* and Katherine Anthony's *Queen Elizabeth,* so that the public was well prepared for the Virgin Queen. Anderson showed his master-craftsmanship by all he left out, rather than by what he included. From the multitude of events which constituted that glorious Age of Elizabeth he selected the single love-affair of Elizabeth and Essex, as good an example of that concentration and delimitation which is of the very essence of perfect dramatic art as one could wish to find. In this choice he is to be compared with Rudolf Besier whose *The Barretts of Wimpole Street,* too, centered about the great love story. The success of Anderson's play was repeated in Vienna where it was produced as the representative American play in an International Drama Festival.

Spurred on by popular approval of his venture into English history, Anderson next produced *Mary of Scotland,* once again playing with the theme of frustration as a source of tragedy. Although democratic America may have no great compassion for Queens as Queens, it can readily understand the pangs of sorrow of a frail and lovable creature, tricked into marrying a scoundrel and finally beheaded by a jealous cousin in fear of losing her kingdom. Stripped of all its royal settings and costumes, *Mary of Scotland* was emotionally stimulating as a human tragedy. An apparently innocent woman was being sent to her death by an unscrupulous, disappointed, barren cousin. That Anderson's portrait was not strictly historical did not seem to matter, for a biographical play need be true not to the facts of history but to the artistic conception of the dramatist and to the facts of human life as most of us know it.

Other queens have not fared so well on the Broadway stage in recent years. Marie Antoinette in the play, *Madame Capet*, although she was played creditably by Eve Le Gallienne and was given a most elaborate setting, even to the extent of redecorating the theatre in the style of Louis Seize, lasted a single week. Possibly the presence of the motion picture at the same time may have kept away that portion of the entertainment-hungry audience which is merely curious about historical figures, and not especially interested in being emotionally stirred by their difficulties. No one could deny that a more elaborate production of Marie Antoinette's milieu could be given in Hollywood than on the largest and best equipped New York theatre.

This leads to the subject of two classes of theatre-goers who attend biographical plays. Some are merely curious to get a peep into the world of kings and the costumes and settings, to hear the words of the monarch or his consort or mistress. Others care for the emotional background of these leaders of nations who want to perceive the "pulse of the machine," who wish to discover what these people were who changed the map of the world, and made history. It is this appeal to the more fundamental emotions which Maxwell Anderson's plays possess to a greater extent than many other biographical dramas.

The representation of great conquerors like Napoleon, great diplomats like Macchiavelli, schemers like Richelieu, and Cesare Borgia may provoke a casual interest but cannot expect to achieve the popular appeal of plays which are based on nobler activities. The latest play about Napoleon which was presented in New York, *St. Helena* (1936), showed a tired and broken-hearted man, more concerned with receiving the plaster-cast of his young son than with his former imperial powers. This play by R. C. Sheriff and Jeanne de

Casalis had the double distinction of Maurice Evans playing the Corsican with his customary excellence, and of being the first play of English authorship in which he was not a frightful master of evil. It was a novel play in many ways since certain aspects of the Emperor's life which are rarely mentioned were given cogency by expert writing and acting. Thus Napoleon's experiences as a gardner, practically unknown to his students and admirers, appeared perhaps for the first time on the stage.

An adequate stage portrait of the Emperor that would approach the position which he holds in the minds of people is almost insuperably difficult. As Clayton Hamilton says, "Napoleon is easily the most dramatic and most theatric figure bequeathed to memory by modern history; yet there is no great play about him." The reason is that . . . "the image in the public mind was bigger before the curtain rose than after it descended. It is always futile, in the theatre, to dissatisfy a high expectancy."

A play about Napoleon on the American stage must face the added difficulty of confronting an audience which lacks the almost idolatrous veneration which the average French audience would have for the

First Consul. Especially in these days a hero whose greatness was built on the blood of myriads and upon waste and destruction would be particularly suspect. Hollywood, ever-sensitive of which way the wind of popular taste is blowing, almost entirely eliminated Napoleon's bloody exploits in *Conquest* and sought to present him as a lover and father. Even his devastation of Europe was explained as part of his grand dream of a United States of Europe. But the public, despite the glamor of the Great Garbo and the undoubted appeal of Charles Boyer, refused to come. The picture was neither an artistic nor a box-office success.

There remain the plays of heroes who did not win battles or conquer nations by wily diplomacy—the victims of social injustice. Two plays have been written about the Scottsboro negroes, whose guilt after litigation of almost ten years is still far from certain. John Wexley's *They Shall Not Die* was called by most critics the greatest play of social criticism of our time. Two plays have been devoted to the tragic Sacco and Vanzetti who were electrocuted in 1927 for a crime which became an international *cause celebre*. Confessions from the guilty persons came too late to help these unfortunate victims of a Red scare hysteria in the Boom days. A year after the event Maxwell Anderson and Harold Hickerson wrote *Gods of the Lightning,* which, though appealing to certain types of audiences, failed to win wide approval. It was perhaps too near the event to permit the playwright to refine his emotions and to turn an event known to everybody into an artistic creation with an existence of its own. The subject would not leave Anderson's mind and seven years later he returned to it in *Winterset,* one of the best of his plays in verse, and perhaps the first play of *social significance* in the metre of Shakespeare's dramas. The Critics' Circle of New York voted it the best play of the year. It is perhaps the first play in which the hero is one long dead, but living in the search for vengeance of the son. As a biographical drama it was unique.

The tragedy of Tom Mooney was the subject of *Precedent.* Twenty years of imprisonment on a trumped-up charge of which all who are not prejudiced now know he was innocent, made an excellent subject for a tragedy of man's inhumanity to man. Arnold Rothstein, a notorious New York racketeer, who was murdered in a hotel room, proved a disappointing subject for a drama despite the presence in the cast of the young lady of his affections. The success of the play about Jesse vealed that New York audiences were still dazzled by the glamor attached to the career of a train-robber while at the same time they were nominating for the office of Governor of the State a man whose main achievement consisted of his convictions of racketeers. How distance lends enchantment to the view!

The lives of actresses and dancers on the stage have not been at all popular. Jeanne Eagels, Isidora Duncan, and Eleanora Duse made colorless dramatic material. Florence Nightingale was not more successful. The authors erred either in presenting well-known facts which could hardly arouse any interest or by attempting to play up the sensational aspects of the lives of their heroines. Biographies and autobiographies can supply the curious with more information and the sensation-hungry with more excitement than any dramatic vehicle.

As one surveys the hundred biographical dramas of the past two decades, certain definite tendencies are clear. There is a greater democracy of subjects. The interest of the audience is lodged in the more human elements and not in the exceptional characteristics of the heroes or heroines. The language of the successful plays is simple, precise, and usually true to the character revealed. Elaborate settings and costumes will not save an uninteresting play about a lifeless character, no matter what his or her position may be in the history text-books. American audiences, especially, are interested in certain of their great heroes who have exemplified the American way of living and thinking. Lincoln is still the most popular subject for drama. The interest in biographical drama, finally, is increasing. The public is eager to understand the men and women who have made history, who have appeared superhuman and yet, who, when the final curtain falls, appear like ordinary human beings, subject to the same emotions and burdened by the same frailties as the rest of us. Nevertheless, the divine spark shone through their humanity and this divine spark has kindled the enthusiasm of the drama-lovers of America.

The Drama of Social Significance

PEOPLE in "show business" say that this is the time for comedies. The Broadway managers tell aspiring young dramatists that they want nothing but comedies. Are these facts to be interpreted from one point of view? For the present writer they are indicative of the end of another theatre cycle, the end of the era of the Play of Social Significance.

Consider the fate of those brave little organizations which strove to convey messages of social import, often of social change and revolution, through the medium of drama. The Theatre Union, which was most pronounced in its leftist tendencies, expired after a brief three-year existence. Such plays as *Peace on Earth, The Pit, Sailors of Cattaro, Stevedore,* and *Mother* were the most courageous examples in modern American dramatic literature of plays of social protest. The Group Theatre, which tried its hand at social drama with the early plays of Clifford Odets (*Waiting for Lefty, Awake and*

Sing, Paradise Lost), later contented itself with realistic studies of life on the Brooklyn water front in Irwin Shaw's *The Gentle People* and the hardly inspiring study of mismating in Clifford Odets' *Rocket to the Moon*. The Provincetown Theatre has been dead since 1931. The One-Act Play Theatre, after considerable propagandizing through the medium of the *One-Act Play Magazine,* expired after an existence of less than a week.

The Theatre Guild has long ceased to be concerned with social plays. The last Shaw opus, *On the Rocks,* was given its American première by the Federal Theatre Project. To all intents and purposes, the ever-buoyant *Pins and Needles,* that freak on Broadway, was about the last remnant of the Drama of Social Significance which assumed at one time such imposing importance, at least in the minds of its supporters.

Newspaper headlines tell us that industrial production is back to the level of 1929, and a parallel might well be formed in our drama. Comedy is booming again. American audiences want to forget in the Theatre. They don't want to be stimulated to thinking about the great social problems of the day. In 1931, Sklar and

Maltz's *Peace on Earth* condemned the munition manufacturers for fomenting wars, and predicted a new war. In 1936, Sidney Kingsley's *Ten Million Ghosts* attempted to dramatize the facts ascertained by the Nye Investigation. *Journey's End* was revived at the beginning of the 1939-40 season. Somerset Maugham's last play, *For Services Rendered*, was a bitter criticism of the futility of the last World War. Yet a second World War began. The Drama of Social Protest has been ineffective in changing the attitude toward war. When the call came, Frenchmen, British, and Germans marched to their appointed positions as they did in 1914. Perhaps there was less band-playing and flag-waving than in 1914, but the Boys got to the Maginot Line and the Westwall just the same. The memories of audiences are very bad.

Another great social problem which the social drama thought it could solve was that of capital and labor controversy. Since Hauptmann's *Weavers* in 1895, dramatists have attempted to open the eyes of their audiences to the misfortunes of the poorly-paid laboring classes. American dramatists have found in the struggles of capital and labor many rich themes for dramatic exploitation. One of the last productions of the Federal Theatre Project was Sklar's *Life and Death of an American*. Some of our greatest contemporary dramatists have seen in the dramatic struggles between capital and labor excellent raw material for dramatic construction. Galsworthy in his *Strife*, John Howard Lawson in his *Processional* and his *Marching Song*, Elmer Rice in his *We The People*, Paul Green in his *Johnny Johnson*, Albert Bein in his *Let Freedom Ring* are but a few of the more significant dramatists who have tried to solve behind the footlights problems which the Knudsens, Lewises, Greens, and Deweys have worked on behind closed doors. The publications of The New Theatre League, last remnant of the far-flung organization which at one time included the Theatre Union in New York and theatres in scores of cities in America as well as other countries are almost all devoted to the problems of the working class.

Yet the era of the mass play about labor seems to have passed. There seems something symbolically ominous in the tragic suicide of Ernest Toller in 1938. This gifted author of *Man and the Masses* and *The Machine Wreckers* was unable to adjust himself to a world in which the masses in certain countries had permitted themselves to be enslaved by a handful of men. If one would examine the glowing encomiums heaped upon Toller's play when it was presented by the Theatre Guild in the early 1920's, one could not help regretting that so many of the hopes held out for mankind and for the drama have been dashed, thanks to the accession to power of a few unscrupulous individuals.

The play about labor would hardly find a commercial producer today. And this does not mean producers are anti-labor. The revue, *Sing Out the News,* written by the authors of *Pins and Needles,* was sponsored in 1938 by Max Gordon, who has sponsored such "artistic" productions as *Ethan Frome* and *Pride and Prejudice.* If the Broadway producers felt that a sufficiently large audience would support a labor play, they would undoubtedly produce one. When Lillian Hellman's labor play, *Days To Come,* was offered by Herman Shumlin in 1936, there were no clamoring unionists who stormed the box-offices, and the play closed within a week.

It seems that audiences, no matter how mature and how devoted to the drama, can stand just so much social drama and then refuse to take more. The hits of the season are plays in which *characters* are developed. Masses have given way to individuals. It is easier for audiences to become interested in individuals who are clearly delineated than in vague groups who are designed to represent certain factions.

All this seems so elementary to the students of the history of the drama. What makes any drama live at any stage in dramatic history? Any student in secondary school will tell you it is *character*. Even in musical comedy the plot is not so important as it used to be. Jerome Kern and Oscar Hammerstein in their last collaboration, *Very Warm for May*, had almost no plot at all. Yet this musicalization of life in a summer barn-theatre was a hit. Such characters as Liz Spofford, the brainless but good-natured patroness, and Ogden Quiler, the well-intentioned dramatic genius who writes what nobody understands, are living human beings and not the standard comics of musical comedy.

Character even in its aberrations occupies the attentions of the dramatists. Sidney Kingsley adapted Millen Brand's *The Outer Room* into a remarkable psychological study. William Saroyan has given us his fine Broadway play, *The Time of Your Life*. His first play, *The Man With His Heart in the Highlands,* had almost no plot at all, but what living characters!

The impecunious poet, his brilliant son, the man with the horn—has our drama seen such fascinating characters in recent years?

Contrast these studies of personalities with such mass dramas as Upton Sinclair's *Singing Jailbirds* (1927), Paul and Clare Sifton's *1931,* John Wexley's *Steel* (1930), and one can readily understand why it is difficult to remember a single character by name or feature, while the characters of John Steinbeck's *Of Mice and Men* come tumbling out upon us. In the early part of the century Emma Goldman wrote her *The Social Significance of the Modern Drama* in which she expressed the hope that the drama would change men's thinking about the great social problems. What a wealth of writing has been devoted to this subject and with what minute results! Consider, for example, all the plays, novels, poems, and polemics that have been written about the first World War. And what do we see after three decades? Can we hope for any change in man's thinking or acting by means of drama?

Bernard Shaw used to think that by ridiculing the stodgy conventions of the British he could shake them out of their habits of muddling through. After fifty years of activity as a dramatist interested in social change he must be disillusioned indeed to find that he was a very popular playwright in Nazi Germany only because he made fun of the British. Perhaps the only one of his plays that will be revivable in the future will be his *Candida,* as pure a study in human character as one can hope for. *Saint Joan* even in Katherine Cornell's splendid revival was not popular and Orson Welles' revival of *Captain Brassbound's Conversion* was an ignominious failure. *On the Rocks* could not get a commercial producer in America.

What is true of Shaw is true of the other great social dramatists of the early part of the century. Although Ruth Gordon revived *A Doll's House,* and Nazimova gave a remarkably vital performance of *Ghosts,* the plays had lost all of their sociological sting and seemed merely vehicles for the stars. It was only their names, not that of the dour Norwegian, which brought in the patrons. Nobody talks about reviving Galsworthy, and few college graduates, who had not specialized in drama, would recognize Echegaray, Sutro, Pinero, or Henry Arthur Jones.

How can we explain the demise of the Drama of Social Significance? No theories about dramatic cycles or business cycles will account for it. Perhaps some elementary facts of human psychology will be sufficient. Their recognition by the young dramatist bent on changing the world might spare him many a heart-ache later when he sees his *magnum opus* close after an extended run of two nights and a benefit preview.

First and foremost, let us admit that social changes cannot be brought about by dramas alone. In college courses of modern drama we are told that Galsworthy's *Justice* changed the prison system of England. It is time for some ambitious student of the drama to investigate the subject thoroughly to discover what really changed it. Off hand, the writer would say that the play may have contributed about one-tenth of one per cent. If the play was so effective in achieving penological reform why did *The Silver Box* do so little for the inequality before the law; *The Pigeon* so little for methods of charity; *Strife,* so little for the labor struggles?

Another fiction perpetrated in drama courses is that *The Barber of Seville* and other French dramas helped to bring on the French Revolution. The connection may seem easy to perceive in text-books, but in real life it is very tenuous indeed. The burden of proof is most definitely upon the theorists who contend that drama can really change people's views or their reactions. This is not to deny the validity of Aristotle's conceptions of the cathartic effect of tragedy in arousing pity and terror. But what a vast difference there is between feeling sorry for a victim of a strike when he is lying dead on the stage (George Sklar's *Life and Death of an American,* 1939) and doing something about the situation! Leaders of the International Ladies Garment Workers Union, which is responsible for *Pins and Needles,* rarely go to plays. At least, we never hear of Mr. and Mrs. John L. Lewis, or Mr. and Mrs. William Green being seen on opening nights. Perhaps the drama of real strikes and real bloodshed is too vivid in comparison with the make-believe drama on the stage to warrant attendance.

As for the drama's effect upon the people's attitude towards war, slums, social problems of all kinds, the honest observer must admit that very little tangible evidence exists to prove a direct connection. Why, for example, did every one of the dozen plays about Nazi Germany fail? Even such playwrights as Elmer Rice (*Judgment Day,* 1935) and Katherine Dayton (*Give Me The Waltz,* 1937) could not succeed. Most critics would say that the public knew so much about the situation that anything seen on the stage would pale into insignificance before the real thing. It was not the dramas about Nazism which shaped the attitude of the American people toward Nazism.

Neither have the dramas about slums done much for slum clearance. It would be interesting to know what Housing Commissioners think about Sidney Kingsley's *Dead End*. It is common knowledge that the moving picture, *Boys' Town,* did more harm than good to the cause of the institution. Have the dramas preaching tolerance like Channing Pollock's *The Fool* and Jerome's *Passing of the Third Floor Back* lessened intolerance? Have any of the great social problems which confront us been brought nearer to a solution by their presentation in dramatic form? As an observer of the drama of the past two decades and of the behavior of our people, the writer is inclined to be skeptical.

A second reason for the demise of the Drama of Social Significance is to be found in the nature of the drama. Its impression may be powerful while the audience is in the theatre, but once out of it all the impression becomes measurably fainter until it diminishes to the characteristic "swell" or "terrible" which run the gamut of the average man's reactions to even the most potent plays. Observers of the effects of plays upon audiences have not paid sufficient attention to the influence of the surroundings. There was perhaps more truth than salesmanship in the early description of the New York Roxy Theatre as The Cathedral of Motion Pictures. There is something about a cathedral (and did not the revived European Theatre begin in the cathedral with the religious plays?) which by its physical presence impresses those who are in it. A play, too, if presented in the proper theatre with the right costumes and settings, will stir a spectator at the time of production, but the impression will wear off with alarming rapidity as soon as the performance is over. Social dramatists who so earnestly hope that their flaming message will sink in and become a part and parcel of the ideology of the thousands of spectators who come night after night might just as well realize now that very little of any play sinks in at any time. An audience comes out with a kind of hazy glow at best.

The third explanation for the social drama's decline has been stated earlier in connection with the study of characterization of the current plays. The social dramas, so earnestly intent on delivering a message, forgot or de-emphasized the characters. It is against the most elementary laws of human psychology to expect an audience to sit at a two-hour lecture (as in Shaw's *Getting Married*) and expect many ideas to be taken away. Any teacher in any school, from elementary to post-graduate, can tell you that ideas can rarely be dispensed *en masse*. If one can get a single idea across in one day—really across so that it becomes a part of the cultural heritage of the students, he is a happy teacher. Even then it may be the original way in which the teacher presents it or the unusual character about whom the idea is related or associated that makes it stick. In other words, not ideas, but characters will remain in the memories of the audience when the curtain falls. If ideas are recalled it will be those voiced by a living, interesting character. This may be very distressing to the idealists and idea-mongers, but why buck a fundamental trait of human beings? If they were really capable of absorbing ideas in masses, would we be living in the confused world of today?

Does this mean that the drama of today and of the future must be simple comedies or spectacles? Hardly. Serious tragedies like Lillian Hellman's *The Little*

Foxes and noble biographies like *Abe Lincoln in Illinois* can pack their theatres. In both cases the characters are the drawing elements. Perhaps our social dramatists need to study the history of the drama and the psychology of the audience before they try to write more plays. Dumas *fils* said that all that one needs to make a play is a platform, two characters and a passion. Nothing is said of social significance and perhaps nothing need be said.

When Ladies Write Plays

SCOTT said of Jane Austen's style that it possessed "the exquisite touch which renders commonplace things interesting." One thinks of this encomium when evaluating the achievements of American women who write plays, and the close kinship between a Jane Austen novel and Clare Boothe's *The Women* is established. In the list of women who have made commonplace things interesting, would be such successful dramatists as Rachel Crothers, Zona Gale, Zoe Akins, Edna Ferber, Lula Vollmer, Rose Franken, Susan Glaspell, Lillian Hellman, Bella Spewack, and a dozen other important playwrights. The time has come to evaluate woman's contribution to the American drama.

The interest of women in the creative life of the stage is almost entirely confined to the twentieth century. No woman wrote drama for the Greeks; we wonder if they even had a word for it. Sappho is known for her odes, and Aspasia may have made enough wise-cracks to make up a Kaufman comedy, but the record says nothing about any woman's play being produced. Along about the tenth century the nun, Hroswitha of Gandersheim, put some Biblical episodes into dialogue form. These are still extant today and show one of the earliest examples of woman's preoccupation with the commonplace. In the seventeenth century in Germany the wife of the famous critic, Gottsched, wrote some plays, for which she still merits a sentence in Meyer's *Konversations-Lexikon*. The French classic dramatists may have been inspired by women, but they thought little of their intellectual accomplishments. Molière poked fun at feminine pretentiousness in his *Femmes Savantes* and *Les Precieuses Ridicules*. The nineteenth century was dull in drama in all respects but women's achievements were practically nil. The present century, however, marks the brilliant efflorescence of women as creative dramatists. By 1929, they had won enough critical acclaim to warrant special mention in Burns Mantle's *American Playwrights of Today*.

In Mr. Mantle's *Honor Group*, which includes O'Neill, Howard, Green, and Kelly, you will find Miss Zona Gale, whose *Miss Lulu Bett* won the Pulitzer Prize for 1921. In the group which includes such prominent playwrights as Channing Pollock, Bayard Veiller, and Samuel Shipman, are placed Miss Rachel Crothers and Miss Zoe Akins, whose dramatization of *The Old Maid* won the Pulitzer Prize in 1934. Other women who were given extended treatment were Lula Vollmer,

Maurine Watkins, Edna Ferber, Fannie Hurst, Mary Roberts Rinehart, Harriet Ford, and Anita Loos. Altogether some fifty-odd women dramatists are discussed. That was the record up to 1929.

American drama advanced as much since that time as it changed from the beginning of the century to 1929. Rare indeed was the visiting foreign actor, producer, or playwright who considered American drama an object worthy of serious discussion twenty years ago. The Theatre Guild was giving us Benavente, Milne, Shaw, Toller, Werfel, Lenormand, but no Americans. In 1937 Werfel came to America to produce his *Eternal Road*. Toller came to America lecturing to eager listeners, telling them why European drama was dead and that American drama was the greatest that was being written today. What part, if any, have the women dramatists played in enriching the American dramatic output to such an extent that it has assumed world leadership?

One could easily list over a hundred names of women who have written successful plays in the last ten years. Burns Mantle has chosen a women's play in almost every one of his annual collections of the ten best plays of the year. Some of these writers, like Miss Crothers, almost invariably get into the annual collection, which is a tribute either to Mr. Mantle's gallantry or to Miss Crothers' literary excellence—which every honest critic has long admired.

The record follows for the women whose plays were considered by Mr. Mantle as among the ten best of the year from 1919 to 1946.

1919   Zoe Akins' *Declassè.*
         Rachel Barton Butler's *Mamma's Affair.*

1920   Gilda Varesi and Dolly Byrne's *Enter Madame.*
         Rachel Crothers' *Nice People.*

1922   Rachel Crothers' *Mary the Third.*

1923   Lula Vollmer's *Sun-up.*

1924   Mary Kennedy and Ruth Warren's *Mrs. Partridge Presents.*
         Edna Ferber's *Minick* with George S. Kaufman.

1926   Maurine Watkins' *Chicago.*

1927   Edna Ferber's *The Royal Family* with George S. Kaufman.
         Ann Bridger's *Coquette* with George Abbott.

1928   Rachel Crothers' *Let Us Be Gay.*
         Sophie Treadwell's *Machinal.*

1930   Rachel Crothers' *As Husbands Go.*
         Susan Glaspell's *Alison's House*

1931   Rose Franken's *Another Language.*

1932   Rachel Crothers' *When Ladies Meet*.

Edna Ferber's *Dinner at Eight* with George S. Kaufman.

1933   Clare Kummer's *Her Master's Voice*.

1934   Lillian Hellman's *The Children's Hour*.

Zoe Akins' *The Old Maid*.

1935   Katherine Dayton's *First Lady* with George S. Kaufman.

Bella Spewack's *Boy Meets Girl* with Samuel Spewack.

Helen Jerome's *Pride and Prejudice*.

1936   Edna Ferber's *Stage Door* with George S. Kaufman.

Clare Boothe's *The Women*.

Jeanne de Casalis' *St. Helena* with R. C. Sheriff.

1937   Rachel Crothers' *Susan and God*.

1938   Lillian Hellman's *The Little Foxes*.

Lenore Coffee's *Family Portrait* with William Joyce Cowen.

Clare Boothe's *Kiss the Boys Good-bye*.

1939   Clare Boothe's *Margin for Error*.

1940   Lillian Hellman's *Watch on Rhine*.

Rose Franken's *Claudia*.

1941   Sophie Treadwell's *Hope for a Harvest*.

1942   Florence Ryerson's *Harriet* with Colin Clements.

1943   Lillian Hellman's *The Searching Wind*.
Ruth Gordon's *Over 21*.
Rose Franken's *Outrageous Fortune*.
Elsa Shelley's *Pick-up Girl*.

1944   Rose Franken's *Soldier's Wife*.

Certain writers like Rachel Crothers, Edna Ferber, Clare Boothe, Rose Franken, Lillian Hellman, almost invariably get into the collection. The sum total of achievement in terms of dramatic art represents in all probability the richest period of literary activity in which women have participated. This is not to be ashamed of. A play which angers Heywood Broun to the extent of compelling him to write a devastating column is not something to be ignored. There have been any number of critics who have said worthy things about *The Women*. No one can question the author's powers of observation, her sincerity and courage, and her command of the English language.

Women have been proficient in certain forms of literature ever since they began writing. They have been weak (perhaps entirely non-existent) in epic poetry, in

an audience for two hours. What is your reaction after seeing *When Ladies Meet* or any other Crothers success? Much ado about nothing. In her play a woman novelist is trying to make up her mind to have an affair. For three acts ladies sit about and make wise-cracks. And after it is all over the wary novelist makes up her mind not to try it. There is your plot. Nothing objectionable in it at all. Like Barrie's plays, it is "inoffensive." Such an experience in the theatre, however, is not the richest the theatre can offer. There is no emotional response to plays like this one; at least, not the response which great drama had from the days of the three great Greeks to our own Maxwell Anderson in his *Winterset*.

Shakespeare did not bother about preserving the conversation and the pretty little wise-cracks of his own time. His language and ideas are for all time. Of course, we cannot expect every woman who writes a play to speak to the ages. Perhaps it is just as well that they don't try to do so. The experience in the theatre might be unendurable. As John Mason Brown says in his *Art of Playgoing,* and as any other intelligent critic can tell you, dramatic entertainment has many varieties and only snobs or fools would confine themselves to high tragedies.

Drama, when it began, was not a realistic portrayal of life. Realism on the stage as a favorite form of dramatic art is comparatively recent, perhaps no more than fifty years old. Our present audiences prefer it to the old-fashioned melodrama and to romantic drama. For every fantasy like Barrie's *Peter Pan* or Anderson's *High Tor* there are twenty or more realistic plays. Audiences responded to the sordidness of Caldwell's *Tobacco Road*. *Dead End*, with its grime and dirt and smut, really delighted the crowds. And *The Women*, with its manicurists, and foundation garments and maternity wards likewise was well received.

Other outstanding realists of the drama of the past years are:

Edna Ferber: *Stage Door, Dinner at Eight.*

Rose Franken: *Another Language, Claudia, Outrageous Fortune, Soldier's Wife, The Hallams.*

Lillian Hellman: *The Children's Hour, The Little Foxes, Another Part of the Forest, Watch on Rhine, The Searching Wind.*

Clare Boothe: *The Women, Kiss the Boys Goodbye, Margin for Error.*

Anita Loos: *Gentlemen Prefer Blondes, Happy Birthday.*

Bella Spewack: *Clear All Wires, Spring Song, Boy Meets Girl.*

Maurine Watkins: *Chicago, Revelry.*

Sophie Treadwell: *Hope for a Harvest, Plumes in the Dust, Machinal.*

Ruth Gordon: *Over 21, Years Ago.*

Clare Sifton: *1931.*

Zoe Akins: *Declassé, The Furies, The Greeks Had a Word for It, The Old Maid, O, Evening Star.*

Susan Glaspell: *Alison's House, The Verge, The Inheritors. Chains of Dew, The Comic Artist.*

Zona Gale: *Miss Lulu Bett, Mr. Pitt*

Katherine Dayton: *First Lady, Save Me The Waltz.*

Ayn Rand: *The Night of January 16, We, the Living.*

Dorothy Heyward: *Porgy, Mamba's Daughters, Nancy Ann, Cinderelative.*

Margaret Ayer Barnes: *Years of Grace, Age of Innocence, Jenny, Dishonored Lady.*

Hagar Wilde: *Made in Heaven.*

Maxine Wood: On Whitman Avenue.

These have all mastered the technique of the drama; they have captured the fleeting words of everyday life; they have been very clever; but they rarely hit the high note of great drama.

No one knows what part of a Ferber-Kaufman play is Miss Ferber's, but a comparison with Miss Ferber's own novels and short stories may give a clue. *Show Boat* has everything that most Americans consider good novelistic art. It has romance, rich enough to survive two movie versions and three Broadway presentations. It is "wholesome." It is colorful. All these adjectives describe the Ferber-Kaufman shows. Consider their *Stage Door*. The authors have certainly caught the language of the stage girls in their rooming house. Perhaps the characters are a wee bit too clever, but we'll forgive that little oversight. Everybody feels perfectly at home in the theatre. Not a single gag, not a single bit of stage lingo but is immediately recognized as familiar. Why? Because we have been fed these stories about stage girls for years on the screen, in magazines, and in other stage vehicles. Mr. Kaufman and Miss Ferber have compounded all the *clichés* about women behind the footlights into their own comedy. There is art of a certain kind in such craft, to be sure; but there is art and Art.

For a few moments in the play a new type of star holds the stage. Now, New York has had all sorts of stars in its day: big, little, wide, slim, white, black, speechless and mellifluous. But this is the first time a neon electric sign came in for its share of applause. Go to a performance of *Stage Door* and try to refrain from applauding that scene in which the girls put bandages on their eyes before they go to bed, and open the window to let in the Broadway melody and the flash of the neon sign. The audience is amused. Like little children who see a Punch and Judy show, the men and women must express their delight in applause.

All this is something new in the history of the theatre. There was a time when "The Play Was the Thing," as you will recall from your Shakespeare. In America during the 1890's the "Star" was the thing and a great actress could fill a theatre for months if she did little more than walk around and ogle the men in the front row. This ecstasy over an everyday occurrence like the flashing of a neon sign is indeed something new, especially since you can hardly walk down a block of Broadway without seeing a dozen of them. Critics may be bewildered at this phenomenon but those who know human nature are not. The average theatre-goer is only a good-natured, hard-working creature, who has in all probability read no portion of Kant in the original. He chuckles with delight at a neon sign because he is in his element there. When the electric sign in Irving Berlin's *Face the Music* (1931) flashed the name Meshbesher across the stage in the same way as the sign on the

Times. Building flashes "All the News That's Fit To Print," the audience almost stood up and cheered. Here was something the people could see for nothing night after night and would not say "boo" over; but put it on the stage and they rock the house with applause.

No amount of criticism of women dramatists for their emphasis on realism will extirpate from their audiences their love of just this kind of realism. Now and then a dramatist like O'Neill or Anderson can compel his audiences to come along with him to his own ethereal heights, but most often the audiences refuse to climb. One would not be surprised to hear many O'Neill fans admit that of all his plays they preferred his *Ah! Wilderness* because it seemed most "natural." Here in this nostalgic comedy of the halcyon days of New England at the beginning of the century, you recognized your own kind. There was no straining one's brain to get at the meaning of things as was necessary in Werfel's *Goat Song* or in Kaiser's *From Morn to Midnight.* Here you could come to the theatre and relax of an evening. The truth is that only a small part of the average audience comes to the theatre not to relax.

Realistic plays relax. They strike home because they are home to you. You hear a character in *Another Language* answer the question "Where do cockroaches come from" with "From the people next door" and you feel happy because you can understand that remark. You heard it or something like it only the other day. "Darned clever of that author to think of it, too", you say. The play is a hit and you tell your friends they must see it.

What made *Abie's Irish Rose* the permanent resident of the Republic Theatre for five years despite the unbroken front of critic disapproval? There was no evidence of great drama in it. The actors were not national figures. The subject matter, however, was familiar. All the gags were hoary with age. The Hebraic father acted as we were taught to believe such fathers should act; the Irish father was the old familiar stage Irishman from time immemorial. The Jewish theatregoers who saw it were amused because they knew the language and loved it. The Irish heard the echoes of their own households. Anne Nichols knew her human beings and decided to humor them to the tune of several million dollars for her own benefit. Why try to give people ideas when they don't want them?

Realism, therefore, is not to be ignored in evaluating the contemporary drama. Such is the preference these days. Twenty years ago Capek's *R. U. R.* could succeed all over the world. It is fantasy pure and simple. More recently the success was *Tovarich,* which is understandable in Berlin, Vienna, Paris, Prague, London, and New York. The women dramatists of America have their ears close to the ground and they can hear very clearly. They may not present those "eternal verities" which seem to be granted to only a blessed few; but they know how to reconstruct for us on the stage our own little houses, and our own little, petty lives, with our worries and cares, and few moments of laughter.

Such an achievement deserves praise. Jane Austen was only a clergyman's daughter, who had few exciting experiences in her life. She was not of gigantic intellect, and she probably did not stand out in a crowd. Dorothy Parker and Dorothy Thompson could probably make her shrink into a corner. Yet her accurate observations of the inanities of the petty people of her own time, published anonymously in her lifetime, have won their way into the hearts of discriminating readers; and her *Pride and Prejudice* as dramatized by Helen Jerome was one of the theatrical treats of 1936. If it is the privilege or the weakness of the daughters of Eve to write faithfully of simple things, our women have availed themselves zealously of that privilege.

The Rediscovery of the Imagination

WHAT is really amazing about the new stagecraft is the willing suspension of disbelief of the enthusiastic audiences. Observers of the American drama of the past two decades, who have heard the lamentations bewailing the demise of the legitimate stage, cannot help feeling elated that at last the spectators of a theatrical production have recovered their imagination. How else can one explain the phenomenal success of *Julius Caesar, The Cradle Will Rock, Our Town,* and *The Shoemaker's Holiday,* and *Joan of Lorraine.*

In the *New York Evening Post* of March 3, 1938, it was stated that a 16mm. movie version of *Caesar* was available for school presentation. What would the moguls of Hollywood, still uncomfortable in their memory of their failure to "sell" Shakespeare to the masses in *A Midsummer Night's Dream* and *Romeo and Juliet* say, if this movie version of Shakespeare with no scenery whatever turns out to be a popular success? Authentic reproduction of a square in Florence and thousands of "extras" in contemporary costumes cannot convey to people the magic of Shakespeare's lines. George Jean Nathan, commenting on Max Reinhardt's production of *A Midsummer Night's Dream* at the Century Theatre in the season of 1928, indicated the futility of approaching with scenic splendor the vision of fairyland which is presented in the mind's eye of a reader who is capable of using his imagination.

The American audience has been accused of many faults, generally assumed to be absent in the more cultured audiences of Europe. It was a favorite charge that our theatre-goers lacked imagination. It was a foreign capital which usually saw the new tricks of production. The revolving stage was used in Berlin long before it was introduced in America. Constructivist settings were popular for years in Russia before one could see them in an American play. Expressionistic dramas were witnessed by European playgoers long before we found them interesting. Does the same situation obtain today?

Where is the imaginativeness of the Twenties which produced in Austria Franz Werfel's *Goat Song* and *Juarez and Maximilian;* which in Germany resulted in Georg Kaiser's *From Morn to Midnight,* in Ernst Toller's *Man and the Masses* and

The Machine-Wreckers; in France, in the psychological subtleties of Lenormand? Clearly the center of innovation in imaginative drama has shifted to America. Perhaps the totalitarian atmosphere was not conducive to artistic ingenuity, as it is not to artistic sincerity. In New York now the artists and the audiences have at last reached a ground of mutual understanding. The dramatist is no longer a mysterious personage known only by his photograph on the playbill. Marc Blitzstein speaks directly to his audiences, Harold J. Rome played his own music in *Pins and Needles.* The "apartness" of the dramatist is no longer emphasized. The artist seeks his inspiration from his audience and the audience is inspired by the artist.

When the historian of the American theatre comes to write the story of this return to the creative imagination, he will have to pay his respects to its earlier manifestations. He will mention *Waiting for Lefty,* of Clifford Odets, who in 1934 made a vibrant play out of a taxi strike in New York. He will go back to 1933 when Sidney Howard made his unforgettable dramatization of a chapter in Paul De Kruif's *Microbe Hunters* and called it *Yellow Jack.* Perhaps he will go back to 1925 when John Howard Lawson's *Processional* disturbed the playgoers with its multi-levelled setting, its incidental music, its bold treatment of hitherto tabooed topics like the Ku Klux Klan and strikes. As the historian will piece together the indications here and there over a period of twenty years, he will be surprised to learn that imaginative dramatists have long been with us. What our drama lacked was *audiences* with imagination.

Pampered by the moving pictures, which not only left nothing to the imagination, but smeared every detail on so thickly that even the ten-year-old could cry out "I get it, I get it," our adults came to expect in the theatre the trappings of a cinema. Even such skilled dramatists as Eugene O'Neill in *Marco Millions* went so far as to have incense burned as a contribution to the atmosphere. Audiences attending on Saturday evenings would imagine that the Theatre Guild had gone Ziegfeld, who had the theatre sprayed with perfume before the performances of *Showboat*.

To a few bold spirits it all seemed tawdry, this loading the stage with objects to oppress the senses. As a result the senses were overwhelmed, but the heart was unmoved. That pity and terror of which Aristotle spoke and about which critics these two thousand years have been arguing, were repressed rather than expressed, because the eye and ear and occasionally the nose (now by scent and in another play by the odor of fried onions) were so occupied that no stimulus could get through to arouse feeling.

Alexander Dumas said that all that was needed for a drama was "four trestles, four boards, two actors, and a passion." Back in 1915 when Susan Glaspell's *Trifles,* still one of the greatest of all one-act plays, was given in Provincetown in an ordinary room, and the audience was moved as only tense drama can move, the words of Dumas were proven true. Today thousands nightly permit themselves to fall under the sway of Shakespeare's verbal magic, which the devastating pedagogical methods of decades have not dulled. How utterly devoid of all knowledge of human psychology was the principle of teaching drama by declaiming of memorized favorite passages to classes incapable of understanding the language!

The course of study prescribed *Julius Caesar* for the last term of elementary school and *Julius Caesar* was "taught." It mattered not that of the students in the class (this refers to New York City) many boys read nothing but Dick Merriwell and Nicholas Carter stories if they ever read at all; that many of them did not speak English at home; that hardly any of them had ever seen a play produced. The syllabus prescribed *Julius Caesar* and *Caesar* you had to learn and like. That *Caesar* was not learned and was indeed hated, we have the unwise planners of the curriculum to thank. Small wonder that the boy of 1916 thought that Shakespeare's plays were a collection of speeches which had to be memorized in a sing-song manner, and which sounded meaningless.

Twenty years have shown how mistaken the curriculum planners were. In 1937 the students in New York City could see a performance of *Julius Caesar* which was perhaps not exactly what Shakespeare intended, but which at least held one spellbound and which made the characters talk like human beings. And now the moving picture of this play is available for classroom use. Though it will lack the magic of the original stage performance, as all artificial reproductions lack the genuineness of living things, yet it will be a worthy substitute, and as an introduction to the Bard's masterpieces, will prove more useful than Hollywood's *Romeo and Juliet.*

One cannot speak slightingly of Hollywood's two herculean efforts to popularize Shakespeare. Yet *A Midsummer Night's Dream* proved a disappointment; neither Max Reinhardt nor William Dieterle would claim responsibility for the fiasco. The vain strivings of James Cagney in a rôle which was utterly beyond his grasp, are indicative of the tense efforts of the movie moguls to bring Shakespeare to Main Street, where the patrons unfortunately prefer Ginger Rogers or Van Johnson. Hollywood needed two glorious failures to learn that Shakespeare cannot be sold by glittering costumes or authentic Renaissance settings or by lovely faces. The words of the Bard go straight to the understanding and the heart of those who are prepared for them. John Barrymore in his radio readings from Shakespearean plays was much more effective than all the glamour of Hollywood in bringing those magic words to millions who may never have understood them before. The heartening success of radio dramatizations from well-known Broadway hits should leave no doubt in our minds that millions are ready for the rediscovery of Shakespeare. He must be rediscovered by many who were inoculated against him with the virus of memorized passages.

Something of the robustness of Elizabethan England was to be found in the Mercury Theatre's second production, Thomas Dekker's *Shoemaker's Holiday*. It was amusing to hear cries of "sit-down strike" from the audience when Mistress Eyre refused at first to accept Hans as a new apprentice. The other apprentices refused to stay and were ready to leave in a body. The spectators again had surrendered themselves to the people on the stage. Surely the plain-board structures and the burlap curtains which divided the stage could not be considered "settings" as we have come to expect them from Donald Oenslager or Jo Mielziner. True, the costumes were of the period, and made the evening's performance colorful. Yet they had a comic meaning all of their own, as Firk's codpiece had a dramatic significance and Hodge's green breeches brought gales of laughter for their own sakes.

Critics have made much of the contemporaneity of comedy as a form of drama. Yet, one of the most entertaining plays in recent years was *Lysistrata,* which ran for almost an entire year. One need not mention the Henry IV plays which have made Falstaff a familiar figure.

Thornton Wilder's *Our Town* is not his first venture in the dramatic form without settings. Having wandered in the mountains of Peru and the hills of Rome and the isles of Greece, he returned in *Heaven's My Destination* to the American scene. Critics were surprised that one who seemed steeped in ancient Greek lore and in South American and Italian life, should find anything to interest him in America. His play,

Our Town, a study of a New England town, with representatives of all the people, was one of the bright stars of a brilliant season. It represents another bit of Americana which is capturing the imagination of our leading dramatists. From John Steinbeck's *Of Mice and Men* to *Our Town* is a stretch of the width of a continent in space and in ideas. Yet, America is large enough and rich enough to contain both environments.

In seeking an explanation for the rediscovery of the imagination as exemplified by these four plays, one must include many factors. For example, the radio play, which insists on the use of the imagination, and which has a large following, according to recent studies, has undoubtedly contributed. The WPA Theatre Project, which brought to many cities legitimate plays where none had been seen for years, has done invaluable service. Small wonder that Orson Welles, who was connected with the WPA production of *Macbeth* and *Faustus* and directed the three Mercury Theatre plays, said recently: "The national theatre is not as remote as some fear. And it won't be a pedestal for stars or a camping ground for amateurs." When this national theatre exists it will find audiences which have been prepared and are eagerly awaiting the project. In 1906 a million-dollar venture in play-merchandising was inaugurated in the hope of interesting theatregoers in American dramatic art. It failed because the masses were not yet ready for such an institution and because mere bigness was substituted for the understanding of the desires and the needs of the audience.

The part played by the American audience in the development of our drama has never been given the attention it deserves. Professor Odell Shepherd has been spending years on a history of American plays from the earliest productions. Professor Arthur Hobson Quinn has written an admirable *History of the American Theatre*. Mr. Burns Mantle has published his *Best Plays* since 1919. Yet, one finds no mention of the history of the American audience. It is obvious to even the casual observer that the audience at *Pins and Needles* is not the audience at *I Married An Angel*. Certainly the people who applaud *The Cradle Will Rock* will not care for *The Circle*. The directors of the Theatre Guild will tell you about their audiences; the Group Theatre had its own followers. The palaces of entertainment, the cathedrals of the cinema, have their patrons.

All of these various bodies of entertainment-seekers come with different purposes: to escape, to laugh, to be aroused, to learn, to get ideas. Most of these purposes were with the theatre from its earliest days. Even the religious awe which greeted such spectacles as *The Miracle* and *The Eternal Road* was of primary concern to the great Greek tragedians. The imagination of the Greeks, which enabled them to dispense entirely with scenery, is now being observed on the Broadway stage. The tragedy of *Caesar*, the biting satire of *The Cradle Will Rock*, the rollicking comedy of *A Shoemaker's Holiday*, the religious faith in *Joan of Lorraine* were all felt without the need of scenic accoutrements. One feels relieved of a burden when only the bare walls and the living actors stand between one and the dramatist's vision. Dramatists in America have a splendid opportunity to create a new and rich art. With audiences prepared and willing to suspend their disbelief, there should enter a new era of native imaginative drama.

INDEX

Index